# A CHOICE OF
# Coleridge's Verse

*Selected
and with an introduction by*
TED HUGHES

*faber and faber*

First published in 1996
by Faber and Faber Limited
3 Queen Square London WC1N 3AU

Phototypeset by Wilmaset Ltd, Wirral
Printed in England by Clays Ltd, St Ives plc

A CIP record for this book
is available from the British Library

ISBN 0-571-17604-6

2 4 6 8 10 9 7 5 3 1

# Contents

# Preface

This selection of Coleridge's verse was prompted by the introductory essay. The essay itself began as a note to another essay about the literary history of what Hopkins called 'sprung rhythm'.*

In the earlier essay, I argued that the metrical characteristics of each definable new phase in English poetry, from Chaucer onwards, can be related to shifts in the dynamic tensions between two metrical traditions, the 'old' and the 'new' – the 'old' originating in what preceded and for a generation or two overlapped with Chaucer, while the 'new' evolved from what Chaucer introduced. And I connected these shifts in the metrical tradition with corresponding shifts in the political, religious and social history of the British Isles.

In sketching, very roughly, the interplay of the two metrical lineages, I had assumed that Coleridge's place in the succession, though it seemed to me important, could be dealt with in a few paragraphs. Once I got to him, I saw this was not possible. Gradually, I realized that his contribution was radical on the largest scale, and that the three great visionary poems – 'Kubla Khan', 'The Ancient Mariner' and 'Christabel' Part I – on which his poetic reputation rests, are the substance of a single extraordinary poetic event – nothing less than the Creation Story of the great song he attempted to sing.

In my Introduction to this selection, I piece together the conception, gestation and delivery of this Creation Story, in Coleridge's writings, and touch on some of its implications. In the course of my argument, I identify a number of Coleridge's other poems by some feature of close kinship with his central vision. Three or four of these, as I try to demonstrate, seem to have been an integral part of the gestation of the vision itself. Others toy with some fragment of the iconic, visionary material, or reflect it obliquely. Each of these pieces is notable for a peculiar poetic

* 'Myths, Metres, Rhythms', in *Winter Pollen* (Faber and Faber, 1994).

vitality, and I make the point that this flashes out, almost inevitably, wherever that visionary core is touched.

Together with the triptych of the three great poems, this supporting cast of more occasional but related verses forms the main part of the present selection. I added a further section of other poems, at the urging of my editor Christopher Reid, partly because these are all interesting in themselves, but mainly because again they illustrate how consistently, wherever the slightest opportunity presented itself, Coleridge's imagination gravitated towards his preoccupation – those obsessive, magnetic symbols of the vision that found its unique expression in the three great poems.

# Introduction:
## The Snake in the Oak

Tho' Christianity is my *Passion*, it is too much my intellectual Passion: &
therefore will do me little good in the hour of temptation and calamity.
 Coleridge, *Letters*

The Tree of Knowledge, from a fifteenth-century Swiss manuscript

# Introductory Note

In my essay 'Myths, Metres, Rhythms' (*Winter Pollen*, 1994), I set Coleridge's 'new principle' of metre within an 'unorthodox' tradition of English prosody, where it conformed to a particular, well-established set of laws (unorthodox, but laws) for manipulating stressed and unstressed syllables throughout the verse line. In that sense, his 'new principle' was far from new, and he was neither introducing a novelty, as he supposed, nor indulging himself in Germanic and wilful caprice, of which he was accused. He was merely reviving, after a 150 year gap, a native mode of verse rhythm, characterized by distinct, objective features, easily identifiable whether in a nursery rhyme or in Shakespeare.

At the same time he was obviously aware, with an intensity that blinded him to the precedents in earlier verse, that his 'new principle' had emerged from a subjective compulsion to search out, within himself, a *new* rhythm – as if the release of what he had to give depended absolutely on his finding that inner 'fountain'* of his own music.

I mentioned that behind the designation 'unorthodoxy', in all the poets who belong to that tradition, there lurks an insistent, peculiar subjective factor – an instinctive attempt to include the experience that orthodoxy excludes, a spontaneous effort to find direct expression for balanced wholeness of being (within which orthodoxy is merely one role among the interplay of many). As I suggested, the contingency of England's political and social

* Claiming his 'new principle' of metre as his own invention, and anticipating the charge that he must have copied it from somewhere, in particular from Walter Scott and Byron (who had in fact copied it from him), he wrote, in the 1816 Preface to 'Christabel': 'For there is amongst us a set of critics, who seem to hold, that every possible thought and image is traditional; who have no notion that there are such things as fountains in the world, small as well as great; and who would therefore charitably derive every rill they behold flowing from a perforation made in some other man's tank.'

history has divided and apportioned the poetic bent of the soul in just that way, between the orthodox and unorthodox traditions of metrical forms. As far as poetry goes, I simplified the division in a rough metaphor about a difficult marriage, where the 'unorthodox' finds itself cast, inevitably, as the turbulent woman.

Even in the most literal sense, this woman does tend to appear, as such, in the works of the distinctive authors of the 'unorthodox' tradition. She is presented either as a real woman, central to the author's life; or in some larger symbolic role; or as a blend of both. In Wyatt, one can find her as a real woman with a very particular personality. In Donne, the undefined women of his love poems are foreground to his deeper struggle with the Great Female – his early Catholicism.*

In Shakespeare, the particular woman of the *Sonnets* is the foreground to the Great Female Catholicism, who is again foreground to the Greater Female of Paganism resurgent.

What the English Church could call Paganism resurgent (rejected or pursued – i.e. prohibited or passionately courted and if possible embraced) has been the dominant theme of European poetry ever since. A curious twin, perhaps, to what the Church calls Godless Science.

In that lineage, Coleridge obviously holds a special place.

This following piece grew out of a remark, in that earlier essay, about the unity of Coleridge's three visionary poems. Here I go a little deeper and argue that the three poems together make a single myth, which is also, as a poet's myths always are (among other things), a projected symbolic self-portrait of the poet's own deepest psychological make-up. Coleridge formulates his myth with extraordinary clarity, coherence, consistency, and with such simplicity that it delivers the full, massive immediacy of its emotional charge.

It is the myth of what made him a poet. In that sense, it is

* Donne's Lament for her 'death' – the Virgin Mary's death – can be read (as Ben Jonson half-divined) into the two extraordinary Anniversary Elegies on the death of the 'virgin' Elizabeth Drury.

specifically the 'creation myth' of his unique music – of the use to which he puts his 'new principle', in fact. It is the myth, likewise, of what destroyed him.

At the same time, given his mind, his curiosity and his reading, it crystallized out of traditional materials and so became the representative myth of a conflict between certain traditions – religious and intellectual – in which Coleridge was a casualty, and perhaps a martyr.

The point I wish to make in this preamble is that though I call the three poems in question a three-act tragic opera, with overture and interludes, Coleridge presents them as one map. In other words, the symbolic world of the three poems has a pictorial simultaneity. The whole thing is there from the first moment, in 'Kubla Khan' – even in the opening five lines of 'Kubla Khan'. The three poems resemble a triple exposure photograph of the same person, the second shot made after zooming in much closer, and the third much closer again.

To describe this gradual poem by poem development of the symbolic map would be straightforward. Once Coleridge's main symbols have been identified, and their place and function in his double nature grasped, everything unfolds like the plot of a play, with the various characters (the symbols and symbolic figures) coming and going, interacting, changing, revealing more of their true nature, as they work out Coleridge's fate. To present that *simultaneity* of the three exposures, however, is slightly more complicated – or rather, it must make some extra demand on the patience of the reader. But if it does, the initial demand is no more than we expect from the opening scenes of a play, where the characters are fully present but still mysterious, moving in all their vigour and yet divulging little of what their significance will be in the play's completed action. The presence of a great reptile, for example, in the first scene, would only be explained bit by bit through the whole play. Our testy demand for instant, full explanation – of every point as it appears – has to be suspended. The following exploration of Coleridge's visionary map requires a similar approach.

# 1 Two Selves

Coleridge was two people. From childhood, throughout life, he had the occasional feeling that he was a 'hive of selves'. But mainly he was aware of being two. 'Who that thus lives with a continually-divided Being can remain healthy?' he cried, in a Notebook entry of 1805. Twenty years later, he identified the two selves precisely:

> Ah, but even in boyhood there was a cold hollow spot, an aching in the heart, when I said my prayers – that prevented my entire union with God – that I could not give up, or that would not give me up – as if a snake had wreathed around my heart, & at this one spot its mouth touched at & inbreathed a weak incapability of willing it away . . . that spot in my heart [is] even my remaining and unleavened *Self* – all else the Love of Christ in and thro' Christ's love of me.

The Christian Self was the one he wanted to be – from the time he was the youngest child of the Vicar (and Headmaster) of Ottery St Mary, to the time he was the ferociously eloquent and informed eight-year-old prodigy, to the time he all but accepted the salaried post of Unitarian preacher in Shrewsbury (in the middle of writing 'The Ancient Mariner'), to the times he increasingly filled his published writing, Notebooks and letters with his Christian preoccupations: increasingly and intensifyingly Christian-Philosophical up to the day of his death. One Christian Self.

On the other hand – that 'unleavened *Self*'. What happened to him? Lying there, immune to Christ's love under the kiss of the serpent – refusing to pray or take any part in the Christian Coleridge's efforts to speak, as Wordsworth did (or as Wordsworth almost did), with 'the language of the whole man'. There in the pious boy. Still there in the fifty-three-year-old Christian ruins of a man.

What was he up to all those years?

'The unleavened *Self*', refusing to have anything to do with

Christianity or its moralizing intelligence, wrapped with a great snake, who constantly kissed him.

Two selves.

## 11 Susceptible Coleridge

Coleridge was besotted with woman. At the same time, few can have so specialized in such terrifying nightmares about such terrifying women. He said he had been his mother's darling. Perhaps he had. The baby of the family – the last of ten. Somehow, very early, he made the connection: woman is the source of all bliss, all love, all consolation. Then everything went wrong. Fighting for mother's exclusive love against seven brothers, he lost. He curled up in the window seat, behind his books, like Eliot's *animula*, and became what also fascinated him, a terrible *Upas Tree* – a logomanic moralist withering every other leaf and sprout within reach.

Very likely, most likely, for a while he truly had been his mother's baby darling. But soon, and from the evidence quite soon, she had to defend his brothers against his intellectual weaponry. In that battle for her exclusive love, which he could not possibly win, he found her repeatedly on their side. One can imagine the schizogenic plot, that he had to live through, on their crowded little rectory stage.

When his beloved father died, STC being only ten, his mother sent him off to the monastic garrison of Christ's Hospital – from which, it seems, he was allowed to return to her bosom only three or four times in the rest of his school days. During this period he shifted his passionate dependence on to his sister, Anne – who then died, after a long illness, just before he left school for university. Later on, to one half-affectionate woman or another, he would say his mother never gave him any feeling of what it was to have a mother. When she died, he neither attended her funeral nor even wrote home (where his eldest brother George had succeeded their father as Vicar).

In his early twenties, the pattern recurred. He lost his first love

7

Mary who seems, at least in his anguished retrospect, to have supplied all his supercharged emotional and erotic needs. But then he let Southey force him (that is how Coleridge himself felt about it, later) into marrying a girl of religious family – his first Sarah. He came to regard his betrothal to her as the worst 'crime' of his life – against her and against himself. Euphoric self-deception, one of his greatest natural gifts, got him through the first two years. But who knows what he was like as a husband? When William and Dorothy Wordsworth rented a house close by, simply to be near him, his marriage began to chafe and suffer. While Sarah nursed baby Hartley, STC was off day and night with his new soul-mate, returning to rhapsodize to her about his new soul-mate's 'exquisite sister' – the new soul-mate he shared with his new soul-mate. Coleridge does not seem to have blamed himself for Sarah's resentment, painful as he found it. But as a gallant and above all honourable fellow, a Christian of enthusiastic, sincere idealism, he kept renewing his efforts of happiness and affection with her. But what did they actually amount to? Opium, too, had entered his life.

And while Sarah waited sourly in the Nether Stowey cottage, what was the submarine and subterranean effect of Wordsworth's sister on her husband – out there under the moons of their mid-twenties, on the high downs over the deep romantic chasms of the Samuel Palmerish, magical, North Somerset Paradise, gazing across the Western Sea? Coleridge already worshipped Wordsworth, calling him the greatest man he had ever met and the greatest living poet. And here was the brilliant, untamed, woodland spirit, with her ethereal nerves, the 'nymph' of the source of Wordsworth's great river, the rapturous sybil of the oracle, the deeply disturbed and disturbing Dorothy.

His mother had sunk into the underground sea. His first love and any other sirens had slid away down the icy caves. This incandescent, twenty-six-year-old spinster – described as 'wild' and 'gypsy' – a moon doomed to the wane, love-sick for everything, for Pan in fact, must have been herself something of a drug, for Coleridge, at that time. She certainly had her effect, probably

8

more by what she evoked than by what she could ever fulfil in person. He dutifully preached on Sundays, but every night of the week, according to the poems he was writing, he dreamed a very different life – as if he had subconsciously emigrated according to his great plan, and had indeed set up his Pantisocratic Paradise (but internally) in the American wilderness, with the aboriginal tribes, on some such half-Goddess of a river as the Susquehanna (he had picked that river purely for the name), among the bellowing of rutting alligators which he had read about in Purchas's account of his travels in the Carolinas (and had duly noted at some length). Somewhere in his imagination, the long-pondered Constitution of Pantisocracy, the ideal society of philosophers, had fallen to pieces, but like a rich humus – i.e. the wild life under it, the 'slimy things with legs' lashed into new vigour, new wild hope in the dark. Apparently, briefly.

## III A Glimpse of the Oak

Wherever he went, Coleridge's overpowering eloquence, what he himself described as the 'velocity' and 'music' of his thought, the voluminous sweep of his torrential ideas, the sheer energy of his mind, became a legend.

At the same time, in his sense of himself he was acutely aware of what he repeatedly referred to as *'an absence of Strength'*. He formulated this idea in all kinds of ways:

> My strength is so small in proportion to my Power – I believe, that I first from internal feeling made or gave light and impulse to this important distinction, between Strength & Power – the Oak, and the tropic Annual or Biennial, which grows nearly as high & spreads as large, as the Oak – but the wood, the heart of *Oak*, is wanting – the *vital* works vehemently but the Immortal is not with it. (Notebook)

Just as obsessive as the idea was that image he had found for *Strength* – the Oak Tree.

The Oak Tree, he felt, was missing.

9

This notion of missing strength was tightly connected to another. What his audience saw as a spectacular aerobatic display of mental activity and language Coleridge himself saw, from the inside, as a fearful escape from something. Again, this notion obsessed him. It came to be part of the constant supervision he kept over all his mental processes – a woeful almost incessant commentary on his exalted facility of intellectual analysis and verbal expression:

> . . . my eloquence was most commonly excited by the desire of running away & hiding myself from my personal and inward feelings, and not for the expression of them, while doubtless this very effort gave a passion and glow to my thoughts. (Notebook)

His perpetual dismay and, often, distress over this particular failing was a permanent emergency, lucid and minutely watchful. He simply accepted that the intellectual self, in his case, had evolved as an escape capsule of some kind, forever scrambling clear of the perilous gulf of his feelings, and soaring somewhere above. Nobody could have studied the escapology of this reflex as fascinatedly as he did. After the first great collapse of his hopes (about 1800, coinciding with Wordsworth's rejection of 'Christabel' from the second edition of *Lyrical Ballads*) he began to detect it in every cerebral flicker:

> why do I always turn away from any interesting Thought to do something uninteresting? . . . is it a cowardice of all deep Feeling, even though pleasurable? (Notebook)

One could collect a small anthology of his comments about just this. They exhale from his constant sense of the misery of it – the encroaching devastations of it.

Yet it is this escape capsule that he lives in, writes all his journalism from, talks to friends, guests and strangers from, sends up his pyrotechnic monologues from, lectures and preaches from, moralizes from and prays in – that he identifies himself with publicly, privately, spontaneously, completely. This fleeing self. And it is this self that lacks *Strength*.

That lacks, in his words, the Oak.

Hence his constant efforts to attach himself to some substitute for this missing Oak Tree: 'My nature needs another nature for its support'. In all his relationships, he was aware of this secret motive and need.

Yet he never seems to have entertained the thought (which nowadays would occur to such a person automatically) that the Oak could be growing well, and the Strength could be deeply rooted, in that very part of himself which he feared so much. And that he lacked it only because it was precisely what he fled from. Perhaps the burning fiery furnace of ever more anguished feeling, which he hadn't the courage (as he admitted) to enter (his 'cowardice of all deep feeling') – perhaps that was the Oak itself in torment. This never seems to have struck him as a possibility. Yet this is evidently what it was. For a very short period, just the one period in his whole life, through the first months of his friendship with Dorothy and William, from the autumn of 1797 to early summer 1798, he was able to confront those feelings and deal with them in their own terms. The result was the three visionary poems. His visionary poetry, as it turned out, was simply this: the language and concentrated, easy courage of mind that could explore, analyse and express the world of his Unleavened Self, of the Snake, of those feelings difficult to face. In that case, if the symbolism of his Unleavened Self were consistent, one could expect to find this visionary poetry centred, something like the cosmology of Norse myth (and something like the inner world common to many shamanic traditions)* on that great tree – specifically the Oak. And also, on the Snake.

* The great axis of the nine worlds of Norse cosmology was *Yggdrasill*, usually described as a cosmic Ash Tree. In almost all shamanic traditions, the tree is somehow central – as the spine common to both this world and the other, or to an upper world, a middle world and a lower world. The concept survives in major religions. Odin, the Norse Allfather, hangs on Yggdrasill for nine nights, a spear through his side,

Through what follows I hope to demonstrate how completely this expectation is fulfilled – in covert form in 'Kubla Khan', openly in the two great narratives, 'The Rime of the Ancient Mariner' and 'Christabel'.

Perhaps one could say, what he had fled from in his earliest days was the tortured tree of feelings that his fixation on his mother had become. As if he had internalized her as the original dragonish Oak. His Strength, grown from her first love, had become his Terror. One can imagine, if she could have assured him of her exclusive, unreserved love, the Oak itself would have seemed to lift him, fearless, into its arms and supportive strength. To re-enter the world of the Oak, and re-unite himself with it, he needed the Oak's Strength. In other words, what he required in his adult life, and what he knew he required above all else, was not merely 'another nature' for the support of his own, but a substitute for her assured love. The assured love of friends, but most of all the assured love of a loved woman. This love would be like the Oak transformed. In one place he actually writes:

> Why is love like an Oak-tree? 1. The myriad roots with the one tap-root deep down as branches high / Earth & Heaven – the present growth still consolidated into the entire trunk – the Nest – the shelter – the leaves pushed off only by the new growth. (Notebook)

---

in shamanic communication with the Giver of Spiritual Gifts, according to his own song:

> I hung in the windshaken tree
> Nine long nights I hung there
> Pierced with a spear
> An offering to Odin
> Myself to myself –

which made Christ a familiar figure to the Norsemen. A rich account of the Tree in shamanism can be found in Eliade's *Shamanism* (details on p. 97). The tight relationship between the Tree and the Serpent (and the Woman) is basic to the old symbolic representations of Goddess religion in pre-Christian tradition: a general account can be found in Joseph Campbell's *Masks of God* volumes (Secker & Warburg).

And for those few months, that mutual infatuation between himself and his revered Wordsworth and the beloved yet untouchable Dorothy somehow supplied his need. Like spiritual parents (Wordsworth automatically took the paternal role, eldest of five orphan brothers and originally intended for the Church), this brother and sister somehow re-created, for Coleridge, in a precarious yet effective way, the primal, unfallen bliss – the 'Nest' in the Oak, where infinite creative courage and acceptance of every truth about himself right back to the womb became child's play.

But the moment passed quickly. The signs are that this 'Nest' was falling to pieces by early summer of 1798. Coleridge records that he and Wordsworth are beginning to find their 'data dissimilar'. As the lease on the Wordsworths' rented house approached its end, inevitably new plans formed. The first edition of *Lyrical Ballads* was completed and off to the printer. With its publication ahead, new adventures opened like a vista. A tour into Germany, the study of German philosophy, beckoned like the next expansive phase of their brilliant, combined advance. As if the seclusion of the last year had been mere preparation. But the circle was obviously broken. Their love-feast of what Dorothy called 'three bodies with one soul' seemed hardly begun, and several years of their now habitual mutual dependence (with passionate episodes) were still to come. But as far as Coleridge's real needs were concerned, in retrospect one can see it was over. Subtle but radical incompatibilities between the two poets, that had been smothered up to now, were waiting only for the public reaction to *Lyrical Ballads*. Then they would be exposed as treacherous reefs. Also, by the time the three of them next came together, in Cumberland, hoping to renew their magic power-circle, Coleridge would be struggling with a new passion. The great love of his life, the second Sara, the sister of Wordsworth's future wife, would be on the scene. And though Coleridge would entertain, for a while, ecstatic dreams of a new 'Nest' in the Oak with this new Sara, there was no practical way in which it could ever happen. Very soon those new hopes would be converted to new, unprecedented agonies, pouring into the awakened terrors of his 'personal and inward feelings' like burning pitch.

Meanwhile that provisional Somersetshire Oak, which had so flourished under the love and husbandry of William and Dorothy, and had given him the nerve to seize the visionary poems, had painfully 'gone'. The actual felling of this particular Oak, the Oak of his inspired months, occurred in 1800 when Wordsworth rejected the completed 'Christabel', and in a note to the second edition of *Lyrical Ballads* dissociated himself from 'The Ancient Mariner' with words that demolished Coleridge's poetic ambitions as well as the poem. After that, Coleridge hesitated to think of himself as capable of writing poetry. 'The poet is dead in me', he wrote a little later, and he meant it. That alternative world of his visionary poetry, which he had penetrated with such difficulty (and so flukishly), had closed again. Or rather, had once again become too terrible to face. When that substitute Oak was felled by Wordsworth's decision and remorseless words, it too toppled into the old internal conflagration, a Burning Oak tossed into a Burning Oak, with such an explosion that Coleridge simply fled. He soared into stratospheric safety (this time for good):

> Poetry is out of the question. The attempt would only hurry me into that sphere of acute feeling from which abstruse research, the mother of self-oblivion, presents an asylum.

From this time onwards, for the next few years, extreme images settle on to the pages of his notebooks, here and there, in smouldering isolation, like sparks from those very flames. Either as a poetic idea:

> Devil at the icy end of Hell warming himself at the reflection of the fires on the ice.

Or as a sudden, exclamatory cry:

> Were I Achilles, I would have cut my leg off to get rid of my vulnerable heel.

Or (perhaps even more startling) as a mad paradox (unwittingly just as self-revealing):

> To be sure, some good may be imagined in any evil, – as he whose house is on fire on a dark night, his Loss gives him light to run away –

Or plain self description:

> To lie in ease yet dull anxiety for hours, afraid to think a thought, lest some thought of anguish should shoot a pain athwart my body, afraid even to turn my body, lest the very bodily motion should induce a train of painful thoughts –

The madness of all that mutilated feeling was the Medusa writhing of the incendiary Oak – the terrifying Hydra of the Oak. It pursued him as a gargoylish woman, a metamorphic dragonish hag into those extraordinary nightmares that made his sleep, quite regularly, nights of screams. These screaming nights of his were also legendary among his acquaintances. A jotted Note for a poem gives a glimpse of what his poetic visionary mythos had become by 1806: 'Death first of all – eats of the Tree of Life / & becomes immortal describe the frightful Metamorphosis / weds the Hamadryad of the Tree / their progeny – in the manner of Dante / –'. But the strength to face and write it was long past.

Much later in his life, towards the end, when the erotic uproar was almost entirely sublimated into his Christian obsessional preoccupation – then once again that divine missing *Strength*, the missing love of his Creatress, of the creative power itself, hovered before him, still inaccessible:

> Elohim = Robora, the Strengths, connected with the image and notion of the TRUNK of an Oak.

*Elohim* means the earliest Jehovah – Jehovah as the 'Lord of Hosts' and Creator of the Universe. The Jehovah of Job as distinct from the later Jehovah of Mercy and Forgiveness. In other words, the term signifies the Jehovah who took over the nature of attributes

15

(in all but sex) of the Great Goddess.* Biblical descriptions of some of His acts reproduce almost verbatim earlier descriptions of the same acts performed by the Great Goddess – Anath (cf. p. 59). The word *Elohim* specifically incorporates, therefore, the Powers of the Great Goddess as suppressed under the name of Jehovah – as in the combination *Yahweh Elohim*. To a degree, then, *Elohim* is 'that other God' who is 'greater than Jehovah' (cf. p. 48), and who turns out to be, in Coleridge's visionary poetic mythos, 'the great, nameless Female' (cf. p. 43), who just as she did in pre-Jehovan Israel inhabits, like a Hamadryad,† the Tree.

The Oak.

This is how it continued to appear to Coleridge's rootless, wind-carried, torrent-hurried, self-anaesthetized bubble of an intellectual, Christian, fugitive Self. In his own words.


## IV The Tragic Opera

The three visionary poems, which came in a hurried sequence, can be read as a single work, a grand opera. 'Kubla Khan' (see p. 117) is like the Overture and a brief Act I.

The Overture states the situation and the themes, in simplified symbolic form, ending with the line:

A sunny pleasure-dome with caves of ice!

The rest of the poem, from the line:

A damsel with a dulcimer

* This Great Goddess incorporates fish and serpent. Moses's magical power (as in his staff) was serpent power. His brazen serpent (Numbers 21: 8–9), that healed any bitten by a snake who looked at it, and was worshipped with burnt offerings, hung in the Temple up to Hezekiah's reformation in the seventh century BC. Jehovah was depicted with snake legs (on amulets) up to the second century BC.
† '(1) *Mythological*: A wood-nymph fabled to live and die in the tree she inhabited. (2a): *Zoological*: A large, very venomous hooded serpent of India . . . allied to the Cobra. (2b): A large baboon of Abyssinia.' *OED*. The Hamadryad was to the tree what the more familiar Naiad was to the stream: a tutelary spirit – i.e. a supernatural attendant protector.

to the end, constitutes Act I. 'The Ancient Mariner' then follows as Act II. And 'Christabel' Part I brings the drama to an end as Act III. Two other poems are germane to the single plot of these three works. One is 'The Wanderings of Cain', which functions both as an Invocation to the whole Opera and a mini-overture to Act II. The other is 'The Ballad of the Dark Ladie', which functions as a mini-overture to Act III and as a bridging passage between Acts II and III.

In the context of this drama the Overture presents a tentative resolution – a truce proposed in trance – of the deadly conflict between Coleridge's two selves. I say 'deadly', considering what the real outcome for Coleridge was to be – which he will describe as 'cutting my own throat', and which he will endure for a lifetime thereafter as an increasingly 'Christian puritan' deadness to the life of the body, of the Oak, and of poetry.

But in Kubla's Paradise, as in a Mandala, the antagonisms are suspended in a pattern of coexistence. This symmetry of polarities within the poem has received plenty of comment. Perhaps the most important one is invisible – as will appear later.

The intellectual aspect of Coleridge's usually dominant Self is manifest in the imperial magnificence of Kubla's pleasure gardens, where everything flourishes, both the perfectly ordered and the utterly wild, under his benign and delighting contemplative supervision – as if this might be a microcosm of his realm. Within this enchanted (as in an opium-trance) consciousness, even the Unleavened Self is permitted to live out its true nature, gratifying its elemental needs. Or at least, it looks as if that is what is going to be permitted. The poem is like the stage ready for action, all but empty of dramatis personae. The sole human presence, as the curtain rises on the gorgeous scenery, is the woman wailing for her demon lover. But her actuality is conjectural, ambiguous: syntactically she is both there and not there. And in any case the lover for whom she wails has not yet arrived.

Nevertheless, her 'savage place', her love-tryst's 'deep romantic chasm', is the spectacular centrepiece of Kubla's paradise gardens, as if he might stroll out along the high terraces with his courtly guests, so that all might be thrilled, in the moonlight, by his preternatural menagerie – this woman's tigerish love-making with a demon in the abyss of the thunderous geyser, while the whole paradise resounds to music produced by natural riverine instruments.

As I say, the Overture presents all this as a joy proposed. It offers the possibility which throughout Acts I, II and III Coleridge will explore, in his doomed attempt to integrate, in some scheme of co-existence, his Christian and Unleavened Selves.

In this Overture the possibility seems to be real (albeit envisioned in trance). But as this first section comes to a close, with rumblings of the action about to begin, the reality intrudes, like thunder in the offing. The ominous lines:

> Kubla heard from far
> Ancestral voices prophesying war!

awaken this dream to the voices of a quarrel that insists on being real and refuses to be resolved or appeased. In the context of the three poems and of this crisis in Coleridge's life, the 'ancestral voices' opposed in war (both historically and psychologically) are those arising from Protestant Christian belief on the one side and those arising from the chthonic and biological energies of Pagan vision on the other. They are the voices of his two selves, now drawing up for the decisive last battle, or rather for the last three engagements of the last battle, which the three poems will enact.

The three Acts are also variations on a single theme: the Female's 'call' to the Unleavened Self and the Christian Self's attempt to reject it. But the intensification, and progressive magnification into close-up, from poem to poem, amounts to a linear dramatic development from beginning to end. The drama is not over, the tragedy not complete, until Coleridge abandons the struggle to undo his Unleavened Self's willing surrender to the 'call' and physically flees – into Germany where the hyper-activated aura of his Christian/intellectual self can protect him, abandoning the Oak, leaving it to burn or smoulder away in agony for the rest of his life.

In the introductory note to these speculations about the unity of the three poems, I suggested that in fact they make a single myth – the myth dramatized in the Three Act Tragic Opera. I further suggested that this myth could be called the Creation Myth of Coleridge's 'new principle' of metre – of the 'music' that he finally delivered in 'Christabel'. Looking broadly at the three poems in which, step by step, this music emerges, a common feature sticks out. Once the poet's two selves have been distinguished and roughly identified, it is clear that each poem revolves around the otherworld female. This semi-supernatural figure modulates from the love-sick mesmeric bringer of ecstatic joys in the Overture and First Act, to the deathly triumphant evil in the Second Act, to the sexually irresistible demon in the Third Act. Or at least these are the faces she seems to present. In each poem this woman is directly, not to say violently, opposed to the Christian values of the Intellectual Self.

But she is further complicated (or simplified, maybe) by one consistent attribute. In her first manifestation, in 'Kubla Khan', she is *the giver of the gift of divine and magical song* that can create an Emperor's paradise in air. In her second manifestation, in 'The Ancient Mariner', she is the giver of a terrifying/beautiful vision that is simultaneously *the strange power of (hypnotic) speech* in which it can be told. And in her third, she is the mesmeric *Lord of Utterance*.

In other words, whatever else she may be, this woman is the spirit of the poet's own *incantatory language*. And Coleridge's Tragic Opera – tragic for him and tragic for her – is at one level (not the least important level) a dramatization of the naked mythos of this 'preternatural' figure. In this way, as I said earlier, it is the 'creation myth' of his 'new principle' of metre (which was the primitive form of Hopkins's 'sprung rhythm').

## v To Paint Kubla Khan's Paradise

Looking at the Paradise depicted in what I called the Overture, one gets the impression of a great sphere, or perhaps an ovoid, broader at the bottom.

The 'sunny pleasure-dome', with its gardens, woods, and river valley, is at the top. A little below, tucked in somewhat under the dome, beneath a forested overhang, removed from the direct sunlight that falls on the dome but mysteriously open to the moon, a deep fold encloses the source of the river. These are the upward, outward features, like the hair and splendid brow, with the spiritual eyes, and beneath it the sensuous perhaps rather crude mouth, of an exotic humpty dumpty.

At the bottom, and within the egg, the 'sunless sea' lies puddled and horribly cold.

From the underside of the dome-capped Paradise at the top, a mass of shaggy, long honeycombs of ice hangs downwards, inside the egg. The drainage system of the River Alph, filtering down through these ice-caves, lengthening them downwards, like icicles in a waterfall, pours into the deathly cold that radiates upwards from the freezing sea beneath. As if Kubla might descend through the basement of his pleasure-dome into these caves, with the right tackle, and peer down through the ice-walls, or directly down through the flues, into the 'measureless' gulf.

A hydraulic system magically syphons renovated fluid up through certain of the caves from the infernal sea, geysers it violently out from the chasm beneath the pleasure-dome, then lets it wander by gravity five miles down the river valley before it dives again through the ice-caves back into the interior and the lifeless ocean below.

With more details, this could be the Indian Miniature painting of the physical appearance of the whole system.

The interest of the place, obviously, lies in the fact that there is more to it. It is a cartoon of Coleridge's psyche. And the river is the Alph. What is so special about the Alph?


Coleridge was a Devonshire boy (and never lost his Devonshire accent, any more than Wordsworth ever lost his Cumberland accent or Burns his Scots). If his grandfather's clan had marched on Exeter, from their high homelands immediately to the west, they would have come down the valley of a stream called the Alphin Brook. But he cannot have meant that.

The Alph is a 'sacred river'. In what way 'sacred'? And how is the 'savage' chasm, from which the Alph erupts so explosively, both 'holy' and 'enchanted'?

And who would that woman be anyway, down there in the dark – wailing for a 'demon lover'? From which pantheon would this 'demon' emerge? One assumes, in Kubla's garden he would not be a sulphurous, Christian, witch's sort of Sabbat Satan. He would be more Oriental, more of a 'god' in mortal disguise, an avatar of Shiva, or at least an unpredictable nocturnal deity, like Psyche's incognito visitant:* a *daemon*, like Socrates' Eros, rather than a *demon*.

Or a dionysiac, possessed man, perhaps. This was the line –

    . . . Woman wailing for her demon lover –

that bowled Byron over, who then persuaded Coleridge (as if against his better judgement, according to Coleridge) to publish the poem (after keeping it unpublished for nineteen years).

Also, there is a mystery about the 'mingled measure' – which can only be music – which comes both from the caves (the ice-cave drainage system) and from the 'fountain' (that erupts 'half-intermitted' and makes rocks dance in air). How do they make music? What sort of music?

* In Psyche's story, the 'latest born and loveliest vision far' on which Keats based his Ode, Psyche's jealous sisters persuade her that her lover, who visits only in the pitch dark and whom she has therefore never seen, is in fact a monstrous snake – rather as Coleridge himself was persuaded, about his visionary inspiration, by his orthodox contemporaries. (And as Lycius, in Keats's *Lamia*, was persuaded, about Lamia herself, by his friend the philosopher Apollonius.) When Psyche lit an oil lamp, to get a peek at her lover as he slept, she saw not a serpent but the great god Eros himself. A hot drop of oil from the lamp of critically sceptical examination fell on his shoulder, whereupon he awoke, and instantly abandoned her. As the Muse abandoned Coleridge.

One thing is certain: any 'mingled measure' that accompanies the pleasures to be had under Kubla's dome must be equally delightful.

So what is this music? Or indeed, what sort of fountain and what sort of caves *make music*?

## VI The Nightingale and the Nocturnal Dinosaur

In *The Road to Xanadu*, John Livingston Lowes dug back through Coleridge's Notebooks and known reading, excavating levels buried in the imagination behind 'Kubla Khan' and 'The Ancient Mariner'.

Poems of this kind can obviously never be explained. They are total symbols of psychic life. But they can be interpreted – a total symbol is above all a vessel for interpretations: the reader fills it and drinks. According to that, what I have to say here may be of use only to me. The only value of these remarks to some other reader may be – to prompt them to fill the vessel up for themselves, from their own sources. Like the variety of potential readers, the variety of potential interpretation is infinite. Lowes's discoveries, then, explain nothing. But they do give interpretation a nudge.

Sticking to the few questions that I asked, one can follow Lowes some way – but then go further, or pick up what he ignored.


Behind the Alph he finds, among other fascinating curios, the Nile – which is 'sacred' *per se*. But is that enough for 'an interpretation'? Then he finds various tributaries for 'holy' and 'enchanted', linked to the river, but trickling also from various mountain paradises. Again, do I want more?

For the 'demon lover' he does not find much that leads anywhere. Nor for the 'wailing woman' – referring only to Coleridge's note about 'wild poem on a maniac', who may or may not have been a woman, and to his other note about a 'maniac in the woods', who certainly was a woman.

His richest findings open beneath the 'mighty fountain'. Direct physical precedents include: springs that explode upwards from a bottomless source, or from an underground sea, having burrowed from some other land, tending to converge again at the source of the Nile.

The fountain's primaeval violence and sound combined have other sources – of which Coleridge took careful note. The most impressive concern the 'alligator hole' in the American wilderness:

> the alligators' terrible roar, like heavy distant thunder, not only shaking the air and waters, but causing the earth to tremble – & when hundreds and thousands are roaring at the same time, you can scarcely be persuaded but that the whole globe is dangerously agitated . . . (Notebook)

That is striking enough. But then Coleridge adds a description of the alligator in rut – an incredible account of convulsive display, thunderous bellowing, belched-out vapours, churning the lagoon – 'all to gain the attention of the favourite female'.

So here is a shattering commotion in a water-hole, a large, erotomanic reptile and the most tremendous of all primordial love-songs – the mating call of a kind of dinosaur, no less.

Lowes merely notes the metaphorical association – as if a poetic metaphor might be nothing but a poetic metaphor. And a reader might well have let it pass easily by: there are no reptiles in the 'savage place' where the woman wails and the Alph erupts. Or are there?

In his Notebook, while he was focused on alligators, Coleridge noted the alligator's eye – 'small and sunk'. A Coleridgean goes direct – as if alerted by a burglar alarm – to Geraldine's eyes in 'Christabel'. On the other hand, 'Christabel' is not 'Kubla Khan' (or at least, not yet).

Keeping those alligators pinned to their place in Bartram, with a small cleft snake-stick (a bit too light for them), Lowes notes (from the Notebooks – immediately following the entry about 'A maniac in the woods' (female) being 'scourged by rebunding [*sic*] boughs') the lines about a nightingale:

> 'Tis the merry nightingale
> That crowds, and hurries, and precipitates
> With fast thick warble his delicious notes,
> As he were fearful that an April night
> Would be too short for him to utter forth
> His love-chant, and disburthen his full soul
> Of all its music! –

which eventually went into Coleridge's poem 'The Nightingale'. Lowes passes lightly. But here, in the exhalations of the underworld from which 'Kubla Khan' rises, the Nightingale's 'fast thick warble', 'that crowds, and hurries, and precipitates', can be heard through the Alph's

> ceaseless turmoil seething,
> As if this earth in fast thick pants were breathing,

and through the wailing of the woman in the dark chasm, uttering her 'love-chant' and striving 'to disburthen her full soul' for her demon lover, and no less clearly through the bellowing of the alligator whose convulsions, by now, are rising more insistently into the boil of the 'mighty fountain'.*

---

* According to several Notebook entries from his time in Malta (1804), Coleridge responded to reptiles as to no other animal. His descriptions of two or three encounters with lizards have a drama, a precision and close-up, riveted, joyous fascination every bit as alive as Lawrence's. He even wants to tame one, and keep it as a pet. But he relishes just as much the hints and rumours of their deadliness. Notice where and how the reptiles enter, in the following Note, during his visit to Sicily:

. . . wound down a road of huge pits, *dimples*, & stairs of Limestone, and came to the view of the arch over the Torrent. Wound down to the Torrent, the River leading our horses thro' such a steep narrow gutter of solid rock / O what a place for Horses / on the Banks 2 High Stones on each side the path, each as large as Bowder Stone / in the Torrent Women & Boys at least 50 washing i.e. thumping & rubbing their cloathes against the Stones in the Torrent. O this savage and unforgettable scene! Huge Stones & huge Trees & small & large Trees and stones & the HIGH HIGH great wall & all one long chamber! &

Perhaps one resists that association between the wailing woman in the dark chasm and the alligator roaring in the Carolinas, even though the treacherous mind has been so quick to spot the link, like a strand of moonlit mucus, between that same alligator's eyes and the eyes of Geraldine. As for the 'slimy things that crawl with legs' in the rotting slime of the Nightmare-Life-in-Death – (the Puritans were right, poetic metaphor is shamelessly promiscuous).

Still, one begins to feel that somewhere between the nightingale's 'fast thick warble', the alligator's volcanic oestrus, the Alph's 'fast thick pants' that shake the earth like the breast of a woman wailing for her demon lover, and the woman wailing under the moon for her demon lover – a song of some kind is twisting into existence, a 'mingled measure' like the braids of current in the Alph itself.

———

the savage women in the Torrent, hairy *men*like legs – Oleander! Ivy!
Myrtle / and all the Pot herbs – lovely Lizards
    The Paradise / . . .

If any other, later writer had made this diary entry – if Ruskin or Tennyson had written it – one could suspect them of plagiarizing consciously or unconsciously the 'savage place' in Coleridge's 'Kubla Khan', where his poem had showed them how to feel and rhapsodize about such a combination of effects. But since it is Coleridge himself writing this, it is not so much self-plagiarism as a more fully explicated gloss on the feelings of that passage in the poem. In other words, it is more explicit about the 'savage women', right there in the water, and introduces the 'lovely lizards' right where, at the peak of his ecstatic response to the whole scene, the reptile ought to appear in the poem but is suppressed. The alligator, and his/her saurian associates suspended as a hidden presence in the poem's 'mighty fountain' are allowed, in the diary version, to come into the open as 'lovely lizards' – immediately producing the cry of consummation, 'The Paradise'. What I am implying here is that exactly the same primal event enthralled him in the Sicilian gorge, recorded in the diary, as produced the vision in the poem. The diary is merely more literal about the actual components.

# VII A Viking Romance

Once all the stops of this particular flute of Marsyas* are brought into play, the fountain of Alph certainly can be said to make music – or to sing. But what about the 'caves of ice'?

Lowes brings a fascinating mechanism of association up behind these caves, again out of Coleridge's reading.

Their music might resound more clearly, though, if they were fitted into the acoustics of the whole Temple – in so far as this egg-shaped Paradise of Kubla's can be called a single Temple-like structure of 'preternatural' 'symphony and song'.

And other answers rise to meet the various questions that I asked, if one resorts to another aid – conveniently close, provided by Coleridge.

For some time before the arrival of 'Kubla Khan' (for my purpose, I assume those commentators (the majority) are right, who date it late October 1797), Coleridge had been toying with the idea of a long poem about 'The excursion of Thor' – 'in the manner of Dante'. Whatever this meant, it meant an activated familiarity with Norse myth. By activated I mean grasped, pondered, ransacked for the workable, set simmering in the creative oven – i.e. the imagination with some purposeful plan for a work to be produced.

One doesn't normally associate Coleridge with the gods of Asgard. On the other hand, through the late 1790s he was preoccupied, if not fascinated, by all things Germanic. Hence Thor – among his very meagre list of planned works (Milton had a list of over ninety).

In any case, even if they were no part of his proposed plot, two

---

* An allusion to the basic, primitive musical instrument of a kind of Pan, which Marsyas was. I refer to Marsyas rather than to Pan because, just as Coleridge's visionary music challenged the Orthodoxy and was defeated, so Marsyas challenged Apollo to a musical contest and was defeated. Marsyas was then skinned alive by Apollo – as one might metaphorically say Coleridge was flayed by the official committee of the Orthodoxy.

stories in particular must have risen from their depths to lie close under it. One – the myth about Thor's fishing for the Midgard Serpent, the giant sea-snake who encircles the Earth at the bottom of the sea and is the sibling of Hel, Queen of the Underworld and Death. The other – the myth about (usually) Hermod's or Odin's descent into Hel's underworld to bring back the dead Baldur – an attempt that was frustrated by Evil herself, the great Mother of the diabolical Loki (who was in turn the father of Hel and the Midgard Serpent).

One can see this steely net of association hanging close to Coleridge's other planned big work – one that he discussed a good deal: *The Origin of Evil*. The ideas might seem more relevant to 'The Ancient Mariner' than to 'Kubla Khan', but once an imaginative idea is on the boil, the steam and flavours leak out at every available orifice. And creative imagination, like evolutionary biology, has a kind of unscrupulous economy about its emergency adaptations. The world plan of Norse myth, matched to that sketch of Kubla's world-egg, amplifies again some of the poem's strongest suggestions and most prominent ideas. Moreover, it shifts the whole complex deeper towards a more radical meaning of 'sacred', and a more universal 'total symbol' of life.

Matching the two as I suggest superimposes the mighty fountain of the Alph on to the 'roaring cauldron', Hvergelmir, which is located at the frozen end of Hel's underworld and is the home of the dragon Nidhogg, the eater of corpses, who gnaws also at the roots of the great tree that holds the worlds together. The cauldron in the underworld boils – and Alph's fountain throws its lid off. This cauldron water belches out from under the roots of the great tree, supplying the waters of the nine worlds, pouring back into sunless and lifeless Hel, and so into Hvergelmir once more, to repeat the cycle.

Two other fountains spring from under the great tree: the waters of Fate, tended by the three Norns, and the waters of Wisdom, from the Orpheus-like or Bran-like severed oracular head of Mimir.

27

These 'preternatural' attributes pour into Coleridge's Alph and will emerge in the two poems that follow.

In particular, they strengthen the conflation of Alph's waters with the waters of a Hell that is half frozen, with the waters of Universal life, with a Queen of the dead and the underworld, who lives with Death (and who is the grand-daughter of Evil), with a corpse-eating giant reptile and by extension with a sea-serpent that fills the sea with its coils. At the same time, they enrich its current with powerful ideas of Fate and oracular speech, knitting the whole tangle inextricably into a great tree which is the backbone and spinal cord of the Universe. The great tree, usually identified in Norse myth as an ash-tree (though not always) would try to become, in Coleridge's imagination, the Oak Tree. Especially in a poem about his chosen hero – Thor, God of the Oak.

Thor did not go on any excursion for Coleridge. The Mariner went on the excursion. Was he a god or tutelary spirit of the Oak?

## VIII Mingled Measures

The 'mighty fountain' that bursts from the 'savage place' is already massively vocal. But the first mention of the music comes almost at the end of this opening Overture, in that phrase

mingled measure
From the fountain and the caves.

These 'caves of ice' also contribute to the pleasures of this Paradise. If anything, the caves are a more marvellous component of the 'miracle of rare device' than the fountain. They are apostrophized, twice, with the same rapture as the 'sunny dome'. Clearly, their part in the 'mingled measure' is important.

These caves seem to function as flutes of some sort, perhaps a gigantic natural organ. And the Alph makes new, other music, a measure to mingle with that of the fountain, as it pours through them, out of the Paradise into the underworld. Coleridge was fascinated by musical instruments of this kind – harps and flutes played on by natural forces.

The concert of water-music begins to come together. The lust-mad giant reptile of the Alph's source (which in the creative cauldron with Coleridge's earlier poetic plans has to share genes with the Norse Nidhogg and the Midgard Serpent, i.e. with the reptile of the underworld's dead waters and with the sea-snake of sea-snakes) will return transmogrified later. But here, in 'Kubla Khan', its roarings are mingled and muffled through the woman's love-sick wails (albeit for a demon) that have been strained through the throat of a heart-bursting Nightingale and, all the time gaining in beauty without losing in volume, are further transmuted, by the technology of the caves, to the measures that accompany the delights of the sunny dome.

In Coleridge's imagination, therefore, the Alph exists, coming and going and at every point of its cycle, as a river of 'holy', 'enchanted', 'demonic', 'oracular', 'fateful', 'elemental', 'love-mad' music and song that emerges from the other world and returns into it.

The presence of the Norse cosmology, in Kubla's Paradise, might be no more than an echo-chamber of harmonies, a scoring for contrabasso, or a shifting gloomy fluorescence in a tapestry that was already rich enough, if it were not for Coleridge's well-established interest in Thor as the protagonist of a long poem 'in the manner of Dante'. That being so, one can reasonably suppose that the hovering co-substantiality of Norse myth, in the whole poem, actually amounts to a structural influence, integral to the dynamic workings of the symbols and to the central meanings of the poetry. This influence becomes much more palpable and evident in 'The Ancient Mariner'.

But this very cosmology points simultaneously to an even more significant model of a divine Paradise – one that must have pressed on Coleridge, in the circumstances, with painful immedi-acy. In this greater model, every element – but especially the river

– is unquestionably sacred. It is the river of absolute sanctity. And though it is not described as a song it is above all the river of ultimate love and of the ultimate Word.

## ix Divining the Spring on Mount Abora

Within this same poem, 'Kubla Khan', the drama now opens with a second, quite separate vision, which constitutes, as I said, a brief Act I of the action proper, beginning with: 'A damsel with a dulcimer'.

All readers recognize the abrupt change of focus and scene at this point. In effect, Coleridge has wakened up. It is as if his Unleavened Self, in the role of the Demon Lover, had arrived too late – just as the Paradise evaporates together with the woman who was wailing for him. Simultaneously, as happens when dreamers wake up, the vision of the paradise, that had seemed actual, is translated into a quite different *memory* which is yet the same. He 'saw and heard' the woman wailing for him in the savage cleft of Kubla's Paradise, but now he remembers her – in a fading image – as 'A damsel with a dulcimer'.

In a desperate attempt to hang on to her, his visionary lens closes in on this woman – apparently to the exclusion of everything else. She fills the foreground. But in this seemingly simplified image all the elements of the first vision are still there, disguised. The woman wailing for her demon lover has modified her style. Her sexual ferocity is now secreted in the irresistible siren-serenade of the black Abyssinian damsel, playing on a dulcimer and singing of Mount Abora. The sunny dome and paradise gardens, with everything contained thereunder, have reappeared as Mount Abora. The river erupting from the chasm has not vanished. It too has been secreted: its source into Mount Abora, its flowing body into the Abyssinian damsel herself, its sound into her song. Lowes has unravelled enough mythic and legendary geography uniting Mount Abora with the Alph, and both with the sources of the Nile, to supply plenty of active if latent meaning clustering around the multiple, interchangeable natures of the river and the woman. Here again are the serpents, the giant slimy things that crawl with legs, bottomless springs, underworld seas, eruptive fountains, etc. – flowing into a river who is also a woman with a musical instrument in one hand and snakes in her crown (as in Apuleius's vision of Egyptian Isis).

The word 'Abora' is as much a key to the code of this second section as 'Alph' (deciphered later) is to the code of the first. And the details go further than Lowes takes them. Coleridge was an addicted punster and manipulator of letters in names. In Abora, whether consciously or not, he unites A + B (= Alphabet) + ora, where 'ora' is the imperative of the Latin 'orare', which means primarily 'to pronounce a sacred formula' or simply 'to pray', producing *oracle*, *adoration*, etc. (or as habitually used by Coleridge in this very form: *ora pro nobis* – 'pray for us'). The root word is the Latin *os* – mouth. The whole hieroglyph, or cryptophone, 'Mount Abora', would be automatically deciphered as a rich pun by, say, Coleridge's close friend and fanatic co-punster Charles Lamb* who, according to Coleridge (Notebook), 'addeth to the Orphic epithetical polynomy of the Natura Naturans the title of the Diva Diapanta Punifica or the Divine All-puntress, and deemeth the Natura Naturata one great complex *Pun*, or Pun of Puns.' In fact neither of them, in each other's company, could have let the opportunity go by. Lamb, if not Coleridge, would read off Mount Abora as 'Mount Alphabeta Oracular Mouth', or 'O Mountain of Alphabet, pray for us!' As if to say 'O Mountain of the Word, pray for us!' Just as we do now.

So Mount Abora becomes the sacred mountain of the divinity within utterance itself. The setting then dramatizes its attributes, just as the setting of the Overture dramatized those of the River Alph. And the shared identity of that river and this mountain becomes even more definite. While the Alph is both the voice of a love-sick woman and a fountain of sacred utterance that issues in a 'mingled measure' of song and music, Abora is a mountain of sacred utterance, the source of a sacred river, that issues through a

* I assume it was Lamb, but it could equally well have been Southey.

bewitchingly seductive damsel in 'symphony and song'. And this second woman, this damsel, converts the listener, Coleridge's Unleavened Self, into the demon that the first woman wailed for in her chasm under her waning (nearly dark) moon.

There is another link, one that must have pressed on Coleridge, in this confrontation, with the sharpness of steel-wire bonds. Among Lowes's findings in Coleridge's immediately relevant much-plundered reading, Mount Abora is associated with a prophesied war that will free all Abyssinia (i.e. all the catchment of the Nile's headwaters) and extend its empire 'as far as Jerusalem'.

In 'Kubla Khan' Coleridge's imagination knew exactly what it was doing. Maybe the ur-form of the two great narratives that follow was what fled when the person from Porlock knocked on the door. Everything in those two poems, as he eventually dug them out, is anticipated here in the Overture – everything essential, as if they were indeed conceived as a single work in parts, like Eliot's *Waste Land*. (Closely related, in fact, to that poem.) Coleridge is somehow aware, in the first five lines of 'Kubla Khan', just what a revelatory event this irruption of the Alph will turn out to be. He recognizes the Alph as the 'birth' of 'demonic' love becoming song. This is the 'nativity', in the sacred epic of his Unleavened Self's adventure as *an inspired incantatory language*. The 'nativity' (in the sacred drama of his own life and fate) of his poetic 'Word'.

Accordingly, this river is aptly identified by the first sound of the Alphabet. But a quite different river is already thundering to be heard through the same letters. This other river appears in the last chapter of The Revelation of St John the Divine, the most famous (and the most familiar in particular to Coleridge) of all Christendom's visions of a heaven on earth. There God speaks through an angel to John saying: 'I am Alpha and Omega'. At this point in the chapter God is speaking in the person of His Son, The Lamb, where 'Alpha and Omega' is the beginning and the end of the life of the Word – of Christ's life. 'Alpha' therefore corresponds to the Nativity of Divine Love. And St John, in his non-opiate trance, hears these words only a few verses after being shown Divine Love not as a God-man being born but as a *river*, pouring out into the world: 'a river of water of life, clear as crystal, proceeding out of the throne of God and of the Lamb.'

In Coleridge's poem, either the river of 'holy' demonic love and the poetic word, which springs from beneath Kubla's pleasure dome and is called *Alph*, has displaced the river of Divine Love and of The Divine Word, which springs from beneath the throne of God and The Lamb and is called 'Alpha and Omega' – or both Paradises are somehow here together and the two rivers are one and the same river. As if there existed perhaps only the one Paradise and river of love and sacred utterance – but reflected differently in each of Coleridge's two selves. In his Unleavened Self it is reflected as it appears in 'Kubla Khan'. But it is reflected (as I said earlier, *invisibly*) in the opposite Christian Self as he knew it in Revelation.

In Revelation St John is surrendering to the 'call' of God. In 'Kubla Khan' Coleridge is all but surrendering to the 'call' of that female. St John is rapt, and Coleridge is likewise rapt. St John is possessed by his Christian Self and is sanctified. Coleridge is possessed by his Unleavened Self and is demonized.

Or rather, not quite. In this first Act, Coleridge has heard the 'call', has had the opportunity, but has let it slip. All he knows is that if only he could 'revive within' himself the damsel's 'symphony and song', he could seize the opportunity and surrender to her 'call' absolutely. He would then be inspired by such a miraculous power of music 'loud and long' that he would be able to recreate

> that dome in air,
> That sunny dome! those caves of ice!

exactly as St John had beheld, just before being shown the river, the Holy City of Jerusalem coming down out of heaven from God – hanging in air like a vast candelabra of precious stones that take ten packed verses to particularize. Then he, Coleridge, would be caught up not into that 'river of the water of life', pouring from beneath the throne of God and The Lamb, but into that pythian gusher of erotic song from the oracular cleft of an African sybil, a voluptuous houri whose voice dements the listener. And this listener, Coleridge himself, understands that he would have drunk his intoxication, his 'milk of paradise' and his 'honey-dew', not from the river and tree of Eden, but from the nectar flow of her song. The whole paradoxical image, in which a demonic woman wails and sings against the invisible Holy City, is a total symbol of the climactic spiritual psychological crisis within the Unitarian Minister Coleridge – where he is longing to submit to the song.

In other words, in this Act I he responds to the 'call' with a will, but then at the last moment he recoils. Or rather, while his Unleavened Self rises into the ecstasy of:

> . . . with music loud and long,
> I would build that dome in air,
> That sunny dome! those caves of ice!
> And all who heard should see them there

his Christian Self reels back in horror, crying:

> Beware! Beware!
> His flashing eyes, his floating hair!
> Weave a circle round him thrice,
> And close your eyes with holy dread.

And the shift demonstrates clearly that Coleridge leaps, in these very lines, from his Unleavened Self to his Christian Self – where he finds himself calling for his Unleavened Self to be exorcized, or at least neutralized like an imp from hell. Coleridge obeys his Christian Self's injunction, the 'call' is rejected, and the poem comes to an end. This is the first of the three circles that he will weave around that strange woman's attempt to emerge and claim him. It is the first skirmish of the aforementioned prophesied war, and with this first victory, the first statement of his tragic choice.

The character-change from the woman of the sacred river to the river-woman of the sacred mountain is curious. Perhaps in the Overture he makes an image of his own destiny, with its 'sunless sea', in tragic foreboding. But in this brief Act I, maybe he interpreted his own case conjecturally, as it might be if he could only fuse his genius somehow with Wordsworth's. Though Wordsworth's indomitable, granitic massif loomed so large eventually over Coleridge's fall, it obviously provided exactly what Coleridge needed, during this first year of their friendship, to buttress his self-confrontation. Just as Dorothy's whisper in his ear lifted his courage. Together, as I have said, those two made a timely Oak Tree. Or instead of an Oak with a Serpent, 'the same only different' – a mountain with a wild nymph. For the time he was composing 'Kubla Khan', 'The Ancient Mariner' and 'Christabel' Part I, his genius really did have the form that it took on here in Act I: a high Mount Abora, a Mountain of the Moon peak of exalted confidence, love and far-seeing clarity, from which the torrent of inspiration poured.

## x  Learning to Fly: First Lesson

The powers that were repulsed in the First Act, by that Christian voice crying 'Beware! Beware!', come back with a vengeance in the Second. Here in 'The Ancient Mariner' they declare war in earnest.

Or the 'call' – from the woman in the 'savage place' and from the Abyssinian maid – rejected in 'Kubla Khan', is presented to Coleridge again. And this time he has no choice. It is no longer a 'call'. It is now a *fait accompli*.

But he has to be dragged out to where he can hear it. His Unleavened Self is whirled helplessly to the battlefield – where his Christian Self will lose. The 'call' takes that form: the announcement of the Christian Self's defeat.

But the whole visionary event, in which he is whirled to the confrontation, had been prepared for in at least three distinct stages. The first, in his early life. The second, in his first attempt to write a large-scale, sustained, mature poem. The third, in his first collaboration with Wordsworth.

The first stage involved his mother and brothers at home in

Ottery St Mary. When he came along, his mother already belonged to his seven older brothers. Their rivalry with him – for her loving attention – was concentrated in the one closest to him in age. This brother, said STC later, 'had a violent love of beating me'. Everything came to a head, as he later described it, when this brother destroyed a special cheese treat that their mother was preparing for STC, who now knocked his tormentor down. In the fight that followed, young STC grabbed a knife to settle things – and was disarmed by his mother. He then fled in guilt, remorse, rage against both brother and mother intense enough to keep him out hiding and sleeping by the River Otter, through a 'dreadful stormy night', till he was finally frozen and too weak to move, by which as he claimed later: 'I was certainly injured – For I was weakly, & subject to the ague for many years after.' He recalled this incident throughout his life, remembering it mainly as an attempt to make his mother miserable, a last resort bid to become her lost but found and now therefore best-loved lamb. Whether or not this was one of those small childhood happenings that affect the whole adult character, it certainly epitomized in extreme form his relationship to his brothers, to his mother, and to the wilderness of stormy nature.

To begin with, it gave him a dramatically staged, sensationally intensified image of the chronic torture of his childhood: the source of human love first reassuring him, then violently rejecting him and replacing him with his rival. According to his own analysis, as his Notebooks witness, he habitually fled from the love-anguish of his 'personal and inward feelings' into his intellectual, moral self, his Christian Self, his aloof and invulnerable sanctuary in the window seat. But on this momentous occasion he fled in precisely the opposite direction. In retrospect, the path he took is familiar. He plunged not into 'abstruse research, the mother of self-oblivion', but into the elemental wilderness of storm and darkness, to find the two things impossible to find in his family and in his ordinary life: first, the superior substitute comforter and strength, who will have to emerge from Nature itself – like God; and second, the mother he has just lost, who must now come searching for him on a deeper level, where brothers do not exist and her love belongs to him alone.

This composite, substitute comforter who will be God, Nature and Mother combined will appear – compelled by his extreme sufferings – and will right every wrong, restore every bliss, supply the perfect love of the very source that created him. She will emerge from the wild Creation itself, out of the storminess of the elements, out of the Otter in spate, wailing for him to return. She will find him, sing him a lullaby that will recreate Paradise, and she will give him her breast of milk and honey-dew. She will speak words that will mesmerize him with bliss as she wraps him in her arms.

His ordeal out there – like a little cub Shaman – freezing to death, will force her to manifest herself and give him all this.

Later on, this strategy cropped up again almost as a fundamental idea, in situations of crisis. At the most superficial level of daydreaming, maudlin self-pity and loneliness, something like it recurred to him now and again, recorded in his Notebooks. On the philosophical level, one could say it was mightily dignified as his Pantisocratic Socialist Utopia – a flight into freedom from competition ('all property in common') and from human malice and strife ('all motive for evil removed') in the American wilderness, where thunder set the alligators bellowing, and the love-mad alligators bellowed like thunder, and the fountain boiled up in a paradise.

On the poetic man-of-letters level it rehearsed itself and brought him relief, so long as he was physically able, in his driven, scrambling flights – more flights than walks – over the Cumbrian or Scottish mountains. On those occasions he grasped and embraced the beauties of the natural world as if only these could console him – though it was never more than invitation and promise, the real thing was always absent. His hectic, headlong abandon was like that of a man searching in despair. And he says it often enough in his Notebooks quite clearly, the more intense the natural beauty the more he is aware – the woman who should be here, and part of this, is missing.

But on the poetic visionary level it lifted him into a paradise in air, where the woman wailed for him, then beckoned and sang to him; it whirled him to the other side of the storm-blast; and it sent him out roaming motherless to pray in the midnight oak forest. Three visionary adventures.

But before these three real flights, it took him somewhere else. It brought him to what I called the second stage of preparation. In this stage, the basic sequence – flight into the wilderness, encounter with the Mother/God/Nature entity, and return to the rectory – was crucially modified.

## XI  Saying Goodbye to Wordsworth

When Coleridge and Wordsworth met they were both Pantheists of a kind. Letting their enthusiasms fly loosely over their basic religious values, both regarded everything as spiritual and tried to believe it inhabited by spirits. Stopping well short of animism, they found themselves entertaining this outlook as a mode, perhaps, of keeping their senses and apprehensions at full stretch. The spirits of Nature were not more individualized or motivated than the spiritual aspect of Nature's elements and features. And all were functionaries of the all-inclusive Universal Spirit, that both poets called God.

They were that aspect of Nature which could be shared by a spiritual human being. Whoever internalized these spirits became to that degree Nature-like. Wordsworth based his religious philosophy on just this. Since he regarded Nature as the natural, the real and the true, it followed that whoever internalized the spirit of Nature partook thereby of the natural, the real and the true – in its Universal spiritualized aspect. Hence:

> One impulse from a vernal wood
> May teach you more of man,
> Of moral evil and of good,
> Than all the sages can.

Coleridge saw more in Nature than this (and was eventually

not sure that he liked what he saw), but in the early days he believed something like the same. Nevertheless, he was not satisfied with it. Wordsworth's approach seemed to him limited. He sensed in it a certain antagonism to the phantasmagoric, to the inner world of symbolism, of dream, of psychic mysteries projected. He criticized it – or Wordsworth's stolid loyalty to it – for its 'meanness'.

Coleridge's idea of 'spirits' included that whole other dimension – the inner world, perhaps even the fringes of a supernatural world, projected by imaginative vision. The inner world not as a climate of feelings that saturated outer events and objects of sense, as with Wordsworth, but as a realm of autonomous dramas, of peculiar states of being, of unfathomable sub- or supernatural personalities, related to the outer world in no simple fashion. This was where he and Wordsworth began to find their 'data dissimilar'.

While Wordsworth was still unknown, and feeling his way, he agreed to call this speciality of Coleridge's the 'preternatural' – as distinct from his own speciality, the 'natural'. He was even willing to indulge Coleridge as far as to sit down and collaborate with him in writing 'The Wanderings of Cain'. Or at least, to make the attempt. And when his invention refused to co-operate, he tried again – much more successfully – with 'The Ancient Mariner'.

But what Coleridge's 'preternatural' world turned out to be was the demonic world of the psyche. And of an extraordinary psyche at that – its spirit-like forces controlled not by the moral will but first and foremost by sexuality, its strange terrors and demands, its dionysiac, elemental music, and the archaic pantheon of energies that emerges with it.

The public reaction to 'The Ancient Mariner', which stood as the introductory poem in the first edition of the *Lyrical Ballads*, helped to wake Wordsworth up to what was happening. By the time Coleridge had finished 'Christabel' Part II, for the second edition, two years later, Wordsworth was fully alerted. And alarmed and repelled. He began to withdraw from both Coleridge and his poems – as Coleridge sensed immediately.

But this occult disposition, from which Wordsworth now stepped back, was already there in the Miltonic poem that Coleridge toiled at for some years before he met Wordsworth – 'The Destiny of Nations – A Vision'.

## xii A Dummy Run on the Astral Plane

'The Destiny of Nations' opens with an address to 'the Word, the Life, the Living God', then presents the Creation as a great machine operated by spirits – where even the bad spirits are good for man because they make him think in spiritual terms and so 'train up to God'.

Where Wordsworth had his mountains for what Keats (with a not dissimilar but less pious idea) called 'mental weight-lifting', Coleridge had already been attracted to the spirit-infested Polar Regions. He describes how the bracing exercise of imagining – internalizing – these supernatural forces exalts the Laplander:

> For Fancy is the power
> That first unsensualises the dark mind,
> Giving it new delights; and bids it swell
> With wild activity; and peopling air,
> By obscure fears of Beings invisible,
> Emancipates it from the grosser thrall
> Of the present impulse, teaching Self-control,
> Till Superstition with unconscious hand
> Seat Reason on her throne.

Coleridge goes on to say how the more frightening the imaginings are, the better they are for the soul, which is sensitized and hurried that much quicker to an acceptance of the 'victorious goodness of high God'. Is this like 'Fear of the Lord is the beginning of wisdom'? What is more revealing is the 'frightening' example that he chooses for illustration to his argument:

> Wherefore not vain,
> Nor yet without permitted power impressed,
> I deem those legends terrible, with which
> The polar ancient thrills his uncouth throng:

(awakening them towards God and Reason)

> Whether of pitying Spirits that make their moan
> O'er slaughtered infants, or that Giant Bird
> Vuokho, of whose rushing wings the noise
> Is Tempest, when the unutterable Shape
> Speeds from the mother of Death, and utters once
> That shriek, which never murderer heard, and lived.

This *Doppelgänger* of the Albatross simply sails up. With foreknowledge of what is to come, one might pause to note that this Giant Bird is an emissary of 'the mother of Death'. In Norse myth, the Triple Grandmother of Hel, Queen of Death, was Evil herself. But this is not Norse myth. And this 'mother of Death', whoever she is, punishes homicides. So Vuokho is the bird form of a kind of Nemesis – a guardian of Divine Law. The bird form of the Goddess of Life and Death dealing out Judgement on homicides. A good spirit or a bad? Coleridge flits away from it lightly. He speeds directly to a passage often noticed in relation to 'The Ancient Mariner':

> the Greenland Wizard in strange trance
> Pierces the untravelled realms of Ocean's bed
> Over the abysm, even to that uttermost cave
> By mis-shaped prodigies beleaguered, such
> As Earth ne'er bred, nor Air, nor the upper Sea:
> Where dwells the Fury Form, whose unheard name
> With eager eye, pale cheek, suspended breath,
> And lips half-opening with the dread of sound,
> Unsleeping Silence guards, worn out with fear
> Lest haply 'scaping on some treacherous blast
> The fateful word let slip the Elements
> And frenzy Nature.

41

A wizard, in a trance, pierces the abyssal sea, to confront a Fury Form. A burlesque rehearsal for the Ancient Mariner's voyage, clear enough. It must have been pointed out, but it seems worth making the point again here: this is a straight transcription of an early ethnological account of the Shaman's flight. From the epic of Gilgamesh onwards, literature is full of mythicized and poetically adapted forms of such flights. But so far as I'm aware Coleridge is the first poet in English to refer to the Shaman's flight as technically such, and to make use of it, even if only in such a straightforward descriptive way, in verse. There is no doubt, in other words, that Coleridge has not merely followed instinct to that general type of experience – as Keats did in 'Endymion', 'Lamia' and 'La Belle Dame Sans Merci' (much influenced by Coleridge's example) – but has lit upon the thing itself, in its real context.

He then goes straight on, and comes to that part of the story which holds – as if he knew it – his own Destiny:

> Yet the wizard her,
> Arm'd with Torngarsuck's power, the Spirit of Good,
> Forces to unchain the foodful progeny
> Of the Ocean stream; – thence thro' the realm of Souls,
> Where live the Innocent, as far from cares
> As from the storms and overwhelming waves
> That tumble on the surface of the Deep,
> Returns with far-heard pant, hotly pursued
> By the fierce Warders of the Sea, once more,
> Ere by the frost foreclosed, to repossess
> His fleshly mansion, that had staid the while
> In the dark tent within a cow'ring group
> Untenanted. – Wild phantasies! yet wise,
> On the victorious goodness of high God
> Teaching reliance . . .

This completes the early travellers' report of the shamanic flight and return. Coleridge wanted a 'terrible' legend, a terrific image, but this is the only one in a poem full of 'terrific images' that is not allegorical. That is to say, it is the only authentic 'preternatural' event in what he regarded, over several years, as his most ambitious poetic work.

His anxious (as if obligatory) attempt to redeem his fascinating plunge into the 'wild fantasy' of his 'terrible legend', by surfacing into a sermon about God's goodness, with assurances that 'heavenly Truth' is 'winning her difficult way', by gradual missionary steps, to convert this wizard, is the first rehearsal of the reflex that will cost him so dearly.

In this passage, the tragic 'double' theology of his two selves comes clear for the first time. The Shaman's flight and return is under the protective power of a good spirit – Torngarsuck, and at the end of the episode Coleridge officially assimilates this good spirit to the coming Jehovah. Meanwhile he characterizes that Fury Form as evil. The creature in the sea's abyss, whom the wizard visited and 'by his enchantments' forced to 'unchain the foodful progeny' – i.e. the sea animals, seals, whales, etc. that normally feed the people – is such a horrible being, such a Queen of Chaos, that her very name, if uttered, would 'frenzy Nature'.

The polarity is conventional. The God who protects the wizard's coming and going and belongs to the upper world is good. The Female Spirit who lives at the bottom of the sea and reigns in the lower world, with power over the sea creatures, is evil. This would resemble the Christian-Manichean division of the cosmos between God and Satan but for that evil Female's anomalous control of the source of food. In every other mythology, this Mother of animals and food is also the Mother of Life, in some form. She is not the opposite of the good God. She actually reigns in his place and antedates him: she *is* the good God, or rather she is the deity of Life and Death, like Job's Jehovah, beyond good and evil.

Coleridge can blame his informant. He gives his source (a history of Greenland), and adds a note:

They call the Good Spirit, Torngarsuck. The other great but malignant spirit a nameless female; she dwells under the sea in a great house, where she can detain in captivity all the animals of the ocean by her magic power. When a dearth befalls the Greenlanders, an Angekok or magician must undertake a journey thither. He passes through the kingdom of souls, over an horrible abyss into the Palace of this Phantom, and by his enchantment causes the captive creatures to ascend directly to the surface of the ocean.

In fact, this is a simplified account of one of the most celebrated of Eskimo flight scenarios, recorded in Coleridge's source by a missionary or other Christian witness who had misinterpreted it. The woman at the bottom of the sea is Arnaquagssak also known as Nuliayuk or Sedna. She truly is the Goddess at the source of things, at the source of the weather and fortunes of the Eskimo hunter's world, and virtually therefore the Goddess of food.* She is a Goddess who – like the Great Bird Vuokho's mother of Death – deals judgement. And here she is dealing judgement. She withholds the animals from the hunters only when some human being has breached a tabu. The Shaman's business is to undo the violation, and secure her forgiveness. She is regarded with terror and awe, but as Job regards Jehovah: and in that sense she can only be 'good' and never 'malignant'.

In spite of this initial misunderstanding, Coleridge has flown unerringly to the deity he needed to find. This account, already as I say central in his work, is enough to authenticate the shamanic flight-path of the Mariner's journey, when Coleridge's point-blank poetic honesty will see through his Christian interpretations and identify that female for what she is.

But then he will scramble out of his visionary moment of poetic honesty as fast as he can. And he will look back towards her, from his Christian sanctuary, as if he had never understood anything, and yet with his scarred retina retaining something, when he remarks in his Notebook (in 1802):

* Further west, in Alaska, she becomes *Niggivik* – literally 'place of food'.

44

Alas! Alas! that Nature is a wary wily long-breathed old witch, tough-lived as a turtle, & divisible as the polyp repullulative in a thousand snips and cuttings, integra et in toto. She is sure to get the better of Lady Mind in the long run & to take her revenge too . . .

'The Destiny of Nations' prepared in this way for the third stage, where Torngarsuck and the Great Malignant Nameless Spirit, confronting each other in bigger and also more familiar roles, brought Coleridge directly to 'The Ancient Mariner'.

## XIII The Symbolic Life

Apart from 'Kubla Khan', between 'The Destiny of Nations' and 'The Ancient Mariner' one more work had to be got through. This provided the third and final stage of preparation for the Mariner's journey.

In October 1797, in the first enchanted surge of his friendship with Wordsworth and Dorothy, Coleridge suddenly felt ready to write his long-pondered 'The Wanderings of Cain'. Very few men have attacked their brother with a knife in a fit of jealous rage, but since he had, the open connection between that and this fragmentary prose poem makes itself.

At the same time, in obvious ways, the strange work is like the ruinous shipyard from which 'The Ancient Mariner' was launched – or rather from which it launched itself.

Coleridge's other much-pondered epic, 'The Origin of Evil', together with his Dantesque 'Excursion of Thor', and that curious project, a long poem about Christian of *The Bounty* ('Captain Bligh! . . . I am in Hell!') all gave way suddenly to a convulsive effort to write out (in a single night!) this titanic fantasia about Cain's murder of Abel and his sufferings afterwards.

Coleridge lived a symbolic life if anybody did – the kind of life in which every event, even the slightest, seems to have the structural rightness and resonance of an image in a deeply organized poem. But nothing in it can have been more vibrantly symbolic than the bizarre situation that he stage-managed on this night, when he persuaded his adored new friend Wordsworth to collaborate in the hand-to-hand re-creation of the primal fratricidal combat between the two sons of Adam – the 'pious' and the 'unleavened'.

It could not have been more pointed if he had chosen the exact anniversary of his earlier attempted fratricide and flight into the night of storm beside the River Otter.

But the external situation, the archetypal psychodrama that he had contrived, was merely apparatus. What Coleridge needed was what it enabled him to bring about: i.e. his first, compulsive step towards what he could no longer avoid – the showdown with *the other*.

Wordsworth was to write Abel's murder, as Canto One. Coleridge had to deal with Cain's guilt in Canto Two. Whoever finished first was to start on the final Canto Three. At top speed, Coleridge produced a prose poem unlike anything else he ever did. Then he discovered that the bemused or unbemused Wordsworth was still staring at blank paper – so the poem was abandoned 'in a laugh'. But it was evidently enough. The necessary step had been taken.

In spite of the Gothic genre operatics, which Coleridge inflated, his figure of Cain emerges with some of the actuality of real vision – hypnagogic and disturbing:

. . . and when Cain, his father, emerged from the darkness, the child was affrighted. For the mighty limbs of Cain were wasted as by fire; his hair was as the matted curls on the bison's forehead, and so glared his fierce and sullen eye beneath: and the black abundant locks on either side, a rank and tangled mass, were stained and scorched, as though the grasp of a burning iron hand had striven to rend them; and his countenance told in a strange and terrible language of agonies that had been, and were, and were still to continue to be.

The whole piece is as close to 'A Memorable Fancy' by Blake as it well could be without actually being by Blake. But more tightly articulated – with a palpably more painful relevance to the emergency of the author's life.

Inevitably Coleridge casting himself as Cain brought into play various aspects of the mutually fascinated but still untested rivalry between himself and Wordsworth, where Dorothy is in the foreground and Sarah with her small son in the background. Divination and prophecy are astir.

Coleridge could hardly, consciously, have supposed that Wordsworth was about to become all older brothers, soon to eject him pitilessly from every kind of love and blessing that he could hope for. But reading the piece now, one can fancy that Coleridge's wishful thinking is in control, and has succeeded, with Wordsworth, in fantasy, where he failed with his brother in reality – killed him for his usurpation.

But then worse pain dawns – as he divines, maybe, that Wordsworth has in truth somehow in some dimension already killed him. At this point, where Coleridge realizes that he is murdered Abel as well as guilty Cain, he drops through into the poem's deeper level – the visionary level, where Cain the 'unleavened' Coleridge has killed the Christian Coleridge, Abel.

Now the narrative becomes peculiar. In the brief Canto that Coleridge composed that night, Cain, persecuted by God, wanders through a forest in torments, until his little son, leading him to where he had found water in a desert, brings him to confront what appears to be the spirit of his slain brother Abel, who is also in torment. Abel then makes the strange statement: 'The Lord is God of the living only, the dead have another God.' And he adds that all who sacrifice to the God of the dead while living shall be wretched, but after death 'their toil ceaseth'.

Wanting only freedom from his torments, Cain now starts searching for this 'God of the dead'. Echoes come back, out of the future, from Nietzsche's *Zarathustra*. He appeals to the spirit who seems to be Abel to lead him to this other God. 'Who is this God of the dead? where doth he make his dwelling? what sacrifices are acceptable unto him? for I have offered, but have not been received; I have prayed, and have not been heard . . .' The spirit then leads him – towards the 'God of the dead'.

The cosmology here, clearly enough, has some resemblance to the Greenland Wizard's, in the division of realms between the two Gods – the God of the upper world being good, the God of the underworld (called a God, not a Devil) still to be assessed. Though Coleridge's note to the passage about the Wizard described that 'other God' as a 'malignant' and 'nameless female', in fact, as I showed she is the salvation of the people – their only hope. Just so here, the one whom Cain now seeks in agony and despair (much as little Coleridge ran off into the night of 'dreadful storm') is simply 'the other God' who can release him from his torments.

That would be enough to suggest how desperately Coleridge's Unleavened Self, the Cain in him, is now bent on finding the equivalent of what the Greenland Angekok found at the bottom of the sea.

There exists a rough sketchy continuation of this story, presumably an outline of the projected Canto Three. In this version, rather as 'The Ancient Mariner' will tell his tale to the Wedding-Guest, Cain tells his tale to his wife. He describes how he found in the desert a Juniper Tree, how he encountered the spirit of Abel, and how he then heard from Abel of 'another being who had power after this life, *greater than Jehovah*' (my italics), and of what followed.

Abel is on his way to offer sacrifices to this other 'greater' God, and Cain allows himself and his son to be led. They come to 'an immense gulf filled with water, whither they descend followed by alligators etc.'. Having gone down through this 'alligator hole', they stand in a vast meadow where Abel offers a sacrifice of blood from his arm. He then persuades Cain to offer up the same, from his son's arm.

Cain is about to obey when a second spirit of Abel – this time the true one – descends from heaven attended by the Archangel Michael, and warns Cain not to offer up his innocent child. The first spirit of Abel now throws off his disguise, revealing himself as an evil demon, and flees pursued by Michael.

The sacrifice has not been made, the other God puts in no appearance – the aborted scenario disintegrates in a jangle of discords. Though it is clearly understood that if Cain had only shed blood from his son's arm, then the 'greater than Jehovah' would have claimed at least Cain's son – Cain's surrogate self. (For the 'child' here one can read simply Coleridge himself who, as he complained, felt always to be 'a boy' – on which he blamed much that went so bitterly wrong with his life.)

The whole work leaves a reader looking expectantly into the distance, across the vast meadow, wondering just what other God that might be, who requires blood from the arm and who is 'greater than Jehovah'. In this context, at least, it could not be the Fury Form or the blessed Arnaquagssak, not quite.

As Coleridge told the story of that night's collaboration in later years, he made it clear that he interpreted Wordsworth's inability to contribute as the great poet's tacit disapproval of the 'exceeding ridiculousness' of the scheme – a spontaneous moral judgement of such crushing authority that Coleridge instantly lost all confidence in this uppermost, most urgent theme of his secret life, and promptly disowned it. When he looked at it through Wordsworth's eyes, it simply shrivelled up, as he says, 'in a laugh' – a laugh which now really did smother the death-cry of Abel.

However, the myth of his destiny, the dilemma that he was going to have to live and die by, did not just leak away into the earth and evaporate under Wordsworth's baleful smile. Not just yet, anyway. It would take a few months. Meanwhile, Coleridge's account of the abandoned attempt concludes jauntily: '. . . and "The Ancient Mariner" was written instead.'

No longer a collaboration, but now with a truly inspired nudge or two from Wordsworth. So, sad as ever but also wiser, Cain re-emerged.

## XIV A Leaden Knock and a Golden Echo

'The Wanderings of Cain' is like Coleridge's first determined effort to confront his Sphynx. Re-enforced by Wordsworth's tremendous electrical field of concentration, and under Dorothy's eyes, he batters at the wall of intellectual ego – to break out and through to the 'other God', using second-hand (obsolete) methods and materials. He fails to get through or even to catch a glimpse of what light there might be beyond.

But as Coleridge seemed to know, the moment was ripe. And this effort, this apparent readiness to sacrifice something, this resounding need, woke something up on the other side. In an unguarded moment, 'Kubla Khan' then floats up out of the abyss (up through that 'immense watery gulf' of the alligators) as an answer, an invitation, even 'a call', from the Sphynx. Redefining the situation in highly original – and uniquely Coleridgean – terms. Presenting the same grisly internecine combat, but as an idealized reconciliation – in a paradisal Mandala, as I described it, beyond the opposites. Or with the opposites only just snarling in at the edges of the picture, like goblins of the *sangsara* on a Tibetan *tanka*, muttering about war.

At the same time, the Christian/Manichean conception of the 'other God' as *evil* – is corrected. This 'other God' now turns out to be a nymph (avatar of a Goddess, lover of a 'demon') of love-madness and of vision-building inspirational song.

Also, as an incidental detail, this 'call' reveals the other nature of the 'alligator hole', no longer a sink-hole of deathly waters, the entrance to the land of the dead, but now the teeming source of biological life, love, song and intoxicating beauty.

According to scholars' favoured dates, 'Kubla Khan' could well have followed 'The Wanderings of Cain', quite closely, in this way.

Then 'The Ancient Mariner' began to emerge in early November (1797).

## xv Torngarsuck meets Arnaquagssak

Using the cave-drawing topographical map that he had already reconnoitred in 'The Wanderings of Cain', and combining it with the rough-old guesswork shamanic flight-path that he had appropriated in 'The Destiny of Nations', Coleridge took off – following his nose.

Anybody can trace the Ancient Mariner's route, station for station, in those two guides – remembering that they were very clear in Coleridge's memory, as he proceeded.

Matching his progress, in this way, it is easy to see that where Cain's nerve failed the Mariner's did not. The Mariner's role model was the Greenland Angekok – perhaps, as spirits go, he was that very Angekok now reincarnated; by great subjective need. But many other shamanic flights – from the poetic record – go with him, like consultants. As soon as he gets well out to sea, the sea takes control. He is whirled by the 'STORM-BLAST' (as prophets are snatched up into heavenly vision) to the encounter with the 'greater than Jehovah'.

The Mariner's vessel enters the ice, which closes around it as a crush of ice cliffs. Scylla and Charybdis, multiplied into a whole seascape. Instead of sailing around the outside of the globe, he has sailed into the inside of Kubla's ovoid cosmos, and here he is in the 'sunless sea', at the bottom of the egg. For continuity's sake (and imaginative economy) huge chunks of the ice that hung under Kubla's paradise and piped Alph's water down to the sunless sea, where it cooled and deepened again, have been torn loose by the torrent and are here floating.

They have not entirely lost their voice, these crags of cave. They are still water of Alph, if transposed – otherworld song frozen and now infernalized. They

> . . . cracked and growled, and roared and howled,
> Like noises in a swound!

The 'mingled measure' regressing, maybe, to the original alligator uproar of the fountain source – the subterranean Hvergelmir, at the frozen end of Hel's underworld, towards which they are now drifting. But the terrible ogress of Coleridge's own regular bellowing 'swound' is maybe not wholly absent.

Some commentators have followed the Mariner's errant course as an example of what could happen to the Western World's maritime expansion when blown off course – a maze of doldrums and reversals, highly interesting, as it was too to Coleridge. But the poem is hospitable to every point of view, in the manner of good symbols.

Just so, as a logged account of a spirit adventure – the spontaneous quest undertaken by every soul in dire need, asleep or awake – the Mariner's course is a straight line to the goal. A beeline to the honey-dew and the crucial revelation. Certainly a dire need for Coleridge.

Since this is one of the few great symbolic poems, not an adventure yarn, we shouldn't be surprised if all the elements and natural features now become hieroglyphs – a picture-language engineering a change of worlds. The ice is the barrier: the perimeter crust of the other world. The presiding symbols in this scene-changing are the sun and the moon.

At this threshold the first world, the sun's world, lies behind, in mist, through which the sun moves hidden. The other world, the moon's world, lies ahead, in 'fog-smoke white' through which 'Glimmered the white Moon-shine.'

Since the sun's world, from which the Mariner brings his glare-goggles of conscience and expectation, and into which he will return, is Protestant Christian, this other world ahead will appear first of all as a Hell (as in 'The Wanderings of Cain').

Every feature of the Mariner's discoveries will be distorted, for the Mariner, in this same warp, by those orthodox goggles (and orthodox readers throughout the poem's history have had a similar problem) – till at one of the high points of the poem, the goggles drop off of their own accord.

And at the same point, as the Unitarian Preacher who has to make his poem acceptable to his congregation and to such unpredictably testy friends and opinion-makers as the minister manqué Southey, Coleridge himself will begin to have problems.

The Albatross is a complicated piece of work. Setting his higher controls aside for a moment, one can say that his role in the shamanic flight – the primitive, biological dream dimension of this excursion – is to serve as Keeper of The Threshold.* He is, in his way, a simple form of the whole vision to come – an ABC form, for the Mariner, the new boy. In that role the bird is like Vuokho – emissary of the Nightmare Life-In-Death: of the putrescent death sea and of the teemingly radiant birth sea. That is his simplest function. So he lets the Mariner through the clashing gates, with a fair breeze, into the otherworld, where the revelation waits. And at this point the Mariner kills him: as if that were the necessary turning of the key.

The ship now emerges from one universe into another (occupying the same space and using the same matter – an idea that interested Coleridge). This is the place 'measureless to man', and the breakthrough is perfectly suggested in the couplet:

> We were the first that ever burst
> Into that silent sea.

Just which Universe this new one is appears now in the sun. It is no longer the worldly sun but – wonderfully startling in its context –

> like God's own head.

That is to say, the earthly and everyday Universe has been displaced by the *sacred* Universe, which is actually a kind of Heaven – a rather horrible heaven at this point, but God is there as if in person, nakedly confronting the Mariner.

* Wherever the quest Hero or Heroine crosses into the other world, or takes the critical step into a forbidden mystery, The Keeper of The Threshold usually appears – most often in the form of a bird, animal or fish, sometimes benign and magically helpful, sometimes terrible and threatening destruction. Either way, directly or indirectly, this creature gives place (by immolation, by self-sacrifice, by transformation, by acting as guide or instructor, etc.) eventually to the prize – as if it were some aspect of that prize, the only aspect of that prize visible to the untransformed adventurer in the opening phase.

It is the sun which is *too dreadfully* like God – as if God glared down into the upstaring face of the transgressor. A kind of guilt, in other words, has projected that alarming extra naked glory on to the sun, like a last warning. And in fact, the sun is already changing into something else. Its dreadful likeness to God's own head is a last admonitory flare-up of its God's-own-headlessness. It no longer belongs to this new Universe – which though it is the sacred Universe is not Jehovah's. This new Universe is ruled, as the poem now goes on to make clear, by a 'greater than Jehovah'. In contrast to the other Universe, which was hidden from its deity by many veils, this new Universe is naked before its deity – too naked, terrifyingly naked.

That extra conflagration in the sun has nothing to do with the killing of the Albatross. Countless folktales follow the same shamanic route that the Mariner follows here. In a great many of them, the animal on the threshold is a standard dramatis persona – as if an animal symbol on the wall of the ovum should confront the sperm. In the typical story of that kind, in this role, the Albatross would have said to the Mariner: 'If you want to go further, and find what you need (the infinitely good thing, the sacred bride, rebirth), you must first kill me.'

No such instructions are forthcoming, in the poem, nor does the Mariner betray any motive for killing the bird. He simply kills it – as if not knowing why. As if, in truth, it had asked him – and he had acted, almost, against his will. Nevertheless, though unaware of the archaic rules, the Mariner has obeyed them, and will be rewarded.

Meanwhile, the sun is changing.

## XVI The Lunar Sun

Kubla Khan's paradise is still undergoing the infernal translation. As in classic hells, this too is half fire, half ice. The 'caves of ice' became a whole Antarctic of 'sunless sea', at the bottom of the world. And the 'sunny pleasure-dome' has become 'a hot and copper sky' with a 'bloody sun at noon' stuck in the middle of it, dead overhead. The Mariner's goggles, one might say (as in 'close your eyes with holy dread'), have inverted all values.

But this sun which was, for a moment there, 'like God's own head', is now not only bloody but 'no bigger than the Moon'.

Within the literal meaning of the very few words used by Coleridge, the glorious briefly-Jehovan-seeming sun has become a different kind of sun-god: a blood-sacrifice god – which is at the same time a terror and a sinister moon.

Looking ahead, you see that within not many verses, having sunk, in an episode of pure nightmare, this hellish moon-like sun has been altogether replaced by the moon – a waning moon already familiar.

Regarding the three visionary works again as one drama, this large transformation of the Mariner's world has obvious parallels in the two other poems. In 'Kubla Khan' the imperial order of the 'sunny dome' yields the foreground and action to the savage chasm where the awesome fountain erupts and the woman wails for her demon lover under the waning moon. In 'Christabel', the moon which is full nevertheless looks 'both small and dull' – as the moaning Geraldine emerges from under the Oak Tree. In other words the moon is full, brilliant and yet, like the eye of the alligator, that Coleridge had so curiously noted, 'small and sunk'. This in turn anticipated the shift from the 'fair, large' and 'glittering', 'bright' eyes of Geraldine to eyes that were

> shrunk in her head,
> Each shrunk up to a serpent's eye

on which the whole uncanny power of that poem turns and slithers into horror.

## XVII The Other God: First Impressions

Through Coleridge's Protestant (sharpening to Puritan) goggles, the Mariner now sees that the 'silent sea' is actually a 'lifeless ocean' – is in fact rotting and burning with death-fires, like a deliquescent grave, reminiscent of Hel's putrid underworld.

Or reminiscent of that 'immense gulf filled with water' into which Cain descended 'followed by alligators etc.'.

Sure enough, there are the 'slimy things with legs' crawling on the 'slimy sea'.

This is the nadir of Coleridge's visionary journey – the point at which Cain had to let blood from his son's arm if he wanted to make contact with the 'greater than Jehovah'. The point at which the Greenland Angekok met that 'great but malignant and nameless Female', alias the Mother of food and of all life, and persuaded her to forgive mankind and permit the life-bringing animals to 'ascend directly to the surface of the ocean'.

On cue, out of the setting sun emerges a woman.

Not wailing for her demon lover, though she is in a savage enough place. And not singing, to a dulcimer, a song that transforms the listener to a demon of ecstatic but forbidden utterance. But the main difference, perhaps, between this woman and those earlier two is in the nature of her 'call'. It is no longer negotiable.

At first, she seems reluctant to reveal herself fully. 'A speck, a mist, a shape' – her ship plunges and veers uncannily in the dead calm. But the moment the Mariner does what Cain dared not do – bites his arm and lets the blood flow – she starts her approach.

The fact that he actually drinks the blood is clearly a sacrament of some kind. In the context – communion with a supernatural being – the blood is the God. That woman coming out of the moony sun that was 'bloody' is the deity of the blood-stream, the river of life.

At the same time he is sacrificing himself to her as an offering – in the sense that Cain's son would have been a sacrificial offering of the child self. And she comes to lap at the blood and to take him.

She emerges from the sun – that was formerly like God's own head, then like the bloody moon, and that is now setting. And this setting sun from which she emerges is seen, and vividly described by the Mariner, as if behind dungeon bars. These bars are formed by the bare bones of the ship that brings her. The image is simultaneously positive and negative. In so far as that ball of bloody fire is her home, it is outlawed and locked up (like Coleridge's Oak), and she comes as if out of its prison, as if freed and at large. In so far as it is still the sun that was like God's own head, it is sinking (giving place to 'the dark'), and is shut away by her emergence, by her taking possession of the Universe that seemed to be his.

She emerges, that is, as the women described in Coleridge's nightmares emerged, and at this point, the Mariner's attitude to her is much the same as the sleeping, sometimes screaming, Coleridge's was to them. She seems wholly negative, utterly horrifying. As in:

> . . . a most frightful dream of a Woman whose features were blended with darkness catching hold of my right eye & attempting to pull it out – I caught hold of her arm fast – a horrid feel – Wordsworth cried aloud to me hearing my scream – heard his cry and thought it cruel he did not come / but did not wake till his cry was repeated a 3rd time – the Woman's name Ebon Ebon Thalud . . .

And several others that he recorded.


## XVIII The Other God's Name

At first, the woman seems to be alone in a skeletal hulk that sails briskly through the dead stillness like the charred coffin ship of a Viking hero in the underworld of Hel.

All at once, it appears that she is accompanied by 'a Death'. Then again both figures seem to coalesce in the one person – a woman of erotic allure whose

> . . . lips were red, her looks were free,
> Her locks were yellow as gold

but who is also, at the same time, in some manner 'a Death' – 'white as leprosy'. The narrator, the Mariner, the inspired poet confronting the very spirit of his inspiration now identifies her, point blank, and with horror, as:

57

> The Nightmare Life-in-Death was she,
> Who thicks man's blood with cold.

So this is the very creature, perhaps, the very snake whose mouth touched the 'cold hollow spot' on young Coleridge's praying heart, and would still be there to touch it on the old Coleridge's praying heart, too. But she also comes straight from 'Kubla Khan'.

Towards the end of this same year, 1798, Coleridge began to make a German vocabulary for himself, in his Notebooks. He subtitles *Part The First* 'names of Spirits, Men, Birds, etc', and the first and only entry under A is

### Alpe: the Nightmairs

Possibly he already knew this word and enters it here as an old favourite. A good part of Coleridge's life seems to have been passed in spectacular nightmares about terrifying usually grotesque women, of the sort I quoted above.* But before he met the

---

* A modern therapist might interpret the dream I quoted above as a desperate attempt, by some supercharged autonomous centre of split-off consciousness in the right hemisphere of the brain to remove by physical violence – by terrorist violence – the over-policing, over-discoursive, censorious vigilance of the left hemisphere of the brain, that was denying it access to life. According to the theory, this would manifest itself (in dream) as a terrible woman attacking the right side of the body – but particularly that capsule of the left brain's vigilant intelligence, the right eyeball. This is how comic cartoon inner scenarios, accompanied by metaphysical terror, and actual physical breakdown, correct the errors of ego – again according to the theory. Debunkers of the theory would say that Coleridge found his right eyelid swollen, when he woke, not as a result of the dream but as the obvious cause of it.

Even so, that woman's name is interesting: *Ebon Ebon Thalud*. Doubtless the hidden associations go deep – deeper than Coleridge himself could have followed them. But right at the surface lie:
*Ebon* = Black
Blackness = (Arabic) sacred wisdom
*Ebon* = (via Latin) 'from good' or 'out of goodness'
As an addicted etymologist, Coleridge, too, would find the following lying right at the surface of *Thalud*:

German term *Alpe*, which unites his nightmare women with both a white mountain, like Abora, and his sacred river Alph, he was as familiar with the Greek root *Alph* meaning 'whiteness' (as with the Latin root *Alb*).

Likewise, he was familiar with *Alphos* – meaning 'leprosy'. And

---

*Tha* is the common stem of Thalassa = (Greek) sea

Thanatos = (Greek) death

Anathema Maranatha = (Aramaic) the

most religiously accursed thing. Used in Corinthians (i xvi:22): 'If any man love not the Lord Jesus Christ, let him be Anathema Maranatha'. In a verse diatribe against titled patrons, improvised into his Notebook two or three years before the nightmare, Coleridge had used the phrase:

> However proudly nicknamed, he shall be
> Anathema Maranatha, to me.

*Maranatha* means: 'Our Lord is come', yet is used as a doubly intensified curse in which the missing word *Anathema* is to be understood – remaining unspoken only because it is so unspeakably unclean. *Anathema* was originally a thing devoted to divine use. Specifically, it was a thing devoted to the Goddess Anatha, in the pre-Jehovan Temple at Jerusalem. More specifically, it was the fee of the ritual prostitutes, given to the Goddess Anatha. The two words together, therefore, resemble a compacted verbal hieroglyph of the religious conflict dramatized in the visionary drama of Coleridge's three poems. The coded reference to that particular Goddess, via that particular paradoxical phrase of blessings inverted into a curse, in the name of this particular nightmare ogress, could hardly be more comprehensively precise.

*Lud* = The Celtic British God Lludd (the eponymous God-King of London, who was also known as Llyr, the original of Lear).

The compound of these particles, 'Ebon Ebon Thalud', is therefore virtually the Nightmare Life-in-Death as the High Goddess of Britain in her Black phase. It is certainly the 'preternatural' female of the visionary poems in her rejected (vengeful) phase. The nightmare occurred in Wordsworth's house, about a month after Wordsworth had rejected 'Christabel', and had effectively ejected Coleridge (so Coleridge himself understood it) from any further creative partnership in *Lyrical Ballads*. It preceded by only days Coleridge's first renunciation (in a letter) of his claims to poetic talent, in the terms (handing over all laurels to Wordsworth, demoting himself to nothing more than 'some kind of metaphysician') that were to harden through the rest of his life.

59

with *Alphitos* – the form of the Greek white-faced Goddess who became a nursery bogey but who *healed* leprosy. He had read all the authors. And he had probably seen the connection made between Alphito and Albina – the Goddess of death and poetic inspiration who gave her name to Albion.

The River Alph who was also the waning moon woman, wailing in the holy chasm, who was the black Abyssinian maid singing of the Moon mountain source and the sacred waters of inspiration, recovers her name here more fully qualified as the Nightmare Life-in-Death, white as leprosy.

Who is also the 'great and malignant Female' who ought to be Arnaquagssak or Nuliayuk or Sedna, mother of the sea-creatures, spirit of the sea, Goddess of Life and Death.

## xix The Ancient Mariner becomes one of the Other God's Creatures

The Mariner's blood-sacrifice, biting his arm and drinking the blood, is followed immediately by the coffin-ship coming along-side and the beautiful woman, throwing dice with death, crying 'I've won!'

What is dramatized here is something that happened long ago. Coleridge's Unleavened Self, as he tells us, always did belong to the coldly kissing reptile enfolding his heart. That sacrifice had been made before birth, when he sipped the milk and honey-dew of the womb. This new biting of the arm etc. is simply the ritualized reaffirmation of what had occurred in the dreamtime.

She always was the winner, the owner. There was never a time when she lost. She had embraced her prize, kissing it with her strange, blood-red mouth, from the beginning. Her casting dice and crying 'I've won!' is again simply reaffirmation of what happened long ago, in the dreamtime.

What is new, and always changing, and always forcing her to drag Coleridge into a new observance of the ritual, a new performance of the *agon*, is the encroachment of the Christian Self – the Christian Self's constantly strengthening opposition to her claim, his constantly renewed and more Godly efforts to wrest the Unleavened Self from her coils, to christen it and to exorcize her.

The Mariner's tale began by her summoning the Unleavened Self, the Mariner, in her STORM-BLAST, from the sphere of the Christian Self's influence. Events up to this 'I've won!' are a progressive stripping away of the Unleavened Self's Christian accretions.

But now her cry 'I've won!' plunges the Mariner totally into her Universe:

> The Sun's rim dips; the stars rush out:
> > At one stride comes the dark;

And the waning moon rises,

> > . . . with one bright star
> > Within the nether tip.

which is the Female with her beloved in her embrace, Coleridge's heart within the curve of the serpent. At the same time the sails begin to drip – as the trees in Paradise might drip with honey-dew. But far from being revived by this magical drench, the two hundred sailors, under the power of that moon, with astonishing suddenness, drop dead.

Which is to say that the Mariner's Christian humanity – the active spirits of his Christian Self's influence – cannot exist in the lunar atmosphere of the Female.

Nevertheless, the Mariner still holds back from total acceptance of her omnipotence. As if the Albatross were still doing the work of a crucifix around his neck. As if its corpse were also the Christ-Crossbow with which he had killed what – when it was alive – was the emissary of the Female. Accordingly, the Mariner undergoes for a while the horror of being a Christian conscience alive in the world of the Goddess. Everything that was Christian is dead around him. But those goggles still on his eyes, insisting on their Christian perspective, will not let anything come alive in the world where they cannot recognize life. Though he has given his blood, i.e. his heart, to that Female, he still cannot surrender a certain dead-at-its-post Christian intellectual militancy, with its Albatross Crossbow Crucifix like a mounted weapon.

When he prays, it is as he describes: he prays to Jehovah. But somehow his Unleavened Self now has such power over his speech that he cannot pray. Nothing comes but a 'wicked whisper', like the 'far-heard whisper' with which the Nightmare Life-in-Death's 'spectre-bark' vanished over the sea. Or like her secret kiss, perhaps.

It is now, as he recognizes the utter emptiness of his prayer to Jehovah, the dry-as-dust dishonesty of it, that his Unleavened Self suddenly takes over. The goggles drop off, as if ashamed. Instantly he recognizes her in the sea-reptiles and watersnakes and finds himself blessing these creatures – blessing the very things that were formerly deathly and loathsome. Without doing more than, as it were, opening his eyes, he is suddenly wholly in her world, overwhelmed by the divine beauty of it.

The Albatross drops from his neck into the sea. In other words, it ceases to be a killed god pinned on a crucifix, and returns to her – perhaps as her newly living child. Instantly, the Mariner falls into a blissful sleep of drinking, like an unborn babe, while the ship, under the control of the spirit of the sea, carries him home.

At this point the Mariner has managed to rid himself absolutely of every Christian vestige, and to give himself wholly to that female, who now turns out to be the Mother of all life, reigning in a vision of beauty and bliss.

But one has to ask, does Coleridge himself know quite what has happened, as he struggles to rig the end of the poem, and negotiate the stages of the Mariner's return to the everyday world? Does he think something wonderful has happened to the Mariner, or something terrible – unspeakable? As the Greenland Angekok of a vessel flies back homeward, towards the old and good God Jehovah/Torngarsuck, Coleridge's own Christian conscience revives belatedly – not the Mariner's but Coleridge's. The Christian Self in him hurriedly takes up the pen.

He now strives to get the boat under the control of good Jehovan or Torngarsuck-like spirits. But they are redundant. Other more profound forces are at work. And something, that the now fully awake Christian Self feels is like a 'frightful fiend', follows close behind, though it is what it always was, that 'wily, long-breathed old witch, tough-lived as a turtle, and divisible as the polyp', the mother of the rainbow sea-reptiles. This Nymph of the waters of Alph, of the ocean of Alph, content to have reaffirmed her claim, now overtakes like a submarine earthquake and sinks the ship, with its corpses of obsolete Christian automata.

## xx The Tongue that Cannot Lie

One prototype Scots ballad behind 'The Ancient Mariner' is 'Thomas Rymer'. In this straight account of a shamanic flight, a renowned Scots Wizard – whose legends still hang around the great startling breasts of the Eilden Hills above the River Tweed – was forcibly carried off, on horseback, by a Nightmare Life-in-Death Fairy Queen, and held for seven years in the underworld. When he returned, his speech – like the Mariner's – had been changed.

In that ballad – one of the greatest, with an especially sinister and unearthly melody – Thomas had been given, against all his protests, the very thing he did not want, and that he knew mankind would not accept: – 'the tongue that can never lie'.

The drama of the end of 'The Ancient Mariner' is created by the effect of the Mariner's 'strange power of speech' on those who hear him. The moment he moves his lips, before he could have told anything of his tale, the Pilot of the boat that rescues him falls in a fit. The Pilot's boy goes crazy. The Holy Hermit, much as advised at the close of 'Kubla Khan', raises his eyes 'in holy dread' and prays, and when he gets ashore he can hardly stand.

Most serious of all is his effect on the Wedding-Guest – who is perhaps Coleridge himself.

It is not merely the difficulty of fitting this vision of the triumph of the Pagan Great Goddess into a Christian conscience and way of life that sends Coleridge on his way 'like one that hath been stunned'. It is the fact that she triumphed. The tongue that can tell only the truth has told him that his Christian life, and the limited cognitive system that goes with it, is a lie.

The pious end of the poem is his hollow refusal of a 'call' he is too late to refuse. He refuses the fact – that his Unleavened Self and his 'Strength' belong to what he sees once more, now that he is back on dry land, as 'the great, malignant and nameless Female'. But refusing a fact is no good. And as instructed at the end of 'Kubla Khan', he can weave this second circle around his possessed Unleavened Self (though the 'flashing eye' has already become a 'glittering eye' and the 'floating hair' a greying beard and the demonic singer, who took up the song of Mount Abora, a loon), but it is quite useless.

The Mariner insists on being heard. The 'sunny dome' and the 'caves of ice' go on being rebuilt – but in Coleridge's infernalized perspective, where the female emerges as a Terror.

And what 'the tongue that can never lie' tells him, and will now go on telling him, about himself, destroys his life.


## xxi  Her Symphony and Song

Except for the very brief 'The Knight's Tomb' and a few lines in 'Lewti', Coleridge's unique music is confined to the three visionary poems. These are his true songs – appropriately, since they constitute the drama of his relationship with his Muse.

'Possessed' by this Muse of Song, he found his pure voice in the ballad form. But not in any old ballad. Only in *her* story. And within the two visionary narratives he developed it into a music so new that he had to apologize for its strangeness and explain it (in that brief introductory note to 'Christabel').

His inspired handling of the old four-line ballad verse – a line of four iambics followed by three, in two pairs, basically rhyming on the short lines – has hardly lacked recognition. The 'strange power of speech', that the Mariner claims has been bestowed on him for the telling of his story, actually is there, in marvellously compelling form.

At intervals, Coleridge introduces an extra four-stress line making an octosyllabic couplet (in all but one case) in the second half of the verse. The musical intensification, and the surge of strangeness, that come with this slight innovation, are easily felt.

It brings an effect of melodic liberation, a sudden surprising wildness, bursting from the tight form.

Again, here and there he introduces an extra syllable or two into the four or three iambics. This is not unknown in traditional ballads.* Still, whenever it occurs here, in 'The Ancient Mariner', it produces what has to be called again a sense of sudden musical liberation, together with an intensification of the uniquely Coleridgean effect. This effect is partly musical, but mainly a characteristic style of simple but hypnagogic imaginative encapsulation, not easy to describe but instantly recognizable:

* What is breaking through into Coleridge's poetry here, as pagan vision and a particular music, has a link with my argument in the essay 'Myths, Metres, Rhythms'. The following, from Robert Burns's 'Scrap Book', is to the point:

There is a great irregularity in the old Scotch songs, a redundancy of syllables with respect to that exactness of accent and measure that the English poet requires, but which glides in, most melodiously, with the respective tunes to which they are set. For instance, the fine old song of 'The Mill, Mill, O!' to give it a plain prosaic reading it halts prodigiously out of measure; on the other hand, the song set to the same tune in Bremner's collection of Scotch songs, which begins 'To Fanny fair could I impart', etc., it is most exact measure, and yet, let them both be sung before a real critic, one above the biases of prejudice, but a thorough judge of nature, – how flat and spiritless will the last appear, how trite, and lamely methodical, compared with the wild-warbling cadence, the heart-moving melody of the first. This is particularly the case with all those airs which end with a hypermetrical syllable. There is a degree of wild irregularity in many of the compositions and fragments which are daily sung to them by my compeers, the common people – a certain happy arrangement of old Scotch syllables, and yet, very frequently, nothing, not even *like* rhyme, or sameness of jingle, at the ends of the lines. This has made me sometimes imagine that, perhaps it might be possible for a Scotch poet, with a nice judicious ear, to set compositions to many of our most favourite airs, particularly that class of them mentioned above, independent of rhyme altogether.

> And a thousand thousand slimy things

or:

> And the rain poured down from one black cloud

or:

> And the bay was white with silent light.

When both couplet and extra syllable occur together, the Coleridgean effect is intensified yet again:

> Like waters shot from some high crag,
> The lightning fell with never a jag

or:

> For the sky and the sea, and the sea and the sky
> Lay like a load on my weary eye

or:

> When the ivy-tod is heavy with snow,
> And the owlet whoops to the wolf below.

Coleridge noticed this. When he started 'Christabel' Part I (before he had completely finished 'The Ancient Mariner') maybe he intended it to be another ballad in ballad form, but in the first verse the new music took over:

> 'Tis the middle of night by the castle clock,
> And the owls have awakened the crowing cock;
> Tu-whit! – Tu-whoo!
> And hark, again! the crowing cock,
> How drowsily it crew.

Then he burst out of the ballad stanza completely – but not out of the ballad mode.

## XXII The Lady Out of the Oak

The action of 'Christabel' Part I is simple and single. Geraldine casts a hypnotic spell over Christabel, seduces and sexually violates her – the poem ending with the seduced folded in the arms of the seducer.

The poem begins where Christabel, going out at midnight to pray under the old Oak Tree for her far-away lover, hears a moaning and finds Geraldine:

> The lady sprang up suddenly,
> The lovely lady, Christabel!
> It moaned as near, as near can be,
> But what it is, she cannot tell. –
> On the other side it seems to be,
> Of the huge, broad-breasted, old oak tree.
>
> The night is chill; the forest bare;
> Is it the wind that moaneth bleak?
> There is not wind enough in the air
> To move away the ringlet curl
> From the lovely lady's cheek –
> There is not wind enough to twirl
> The one red leaf, the last of its clan,
> That dances as often as dance it can,
> Hanging so light, and hanging so high,
> On the topmost twig that looks up at the sky.
>
> Hush, beating heart of Christabel!
> Jesu, Maria, shield her well!

The mesmeric passes of these lines prepare the reader for the strange climax of the poem, in which Geraldine reveals the uncanny nature of her power over Christabel. I mentioned earlier that the preternatural woman in each of the three visionary poems is the spirit of a particular kind of utterance. I called her the spirit of Coleridge's *incantatory language*. She was Alph, the river of erotic and sacred song. She was the Abyssinian maid whose song demonized the listener. She was the Nightmare Life-in-Death alias Heaven's Mother alias Arnaquagssak who freed the Mariner from dumbness only when he sacrificed to her his own blood (drinking her in his own blood as it might be communion wine). And she is now the reptilian woman (Coleridge takes pains to let his reader know that) out of Oak, whose words mesmerize the Christian Self – or mesmerize the 'soul' of the Christian Self in the person of Christabel. In each case, this woman's utterance attempts to overpower or does overpower, the Christian Self. In 'Kubla Khan' the Christian Self has to weave a circle around the effects of her song, and so exorcize her. In 'The Ancient Mariner' she overpowered the Christian Self completely: the Mariner is whisked back to the world of Christian values as the mad relic of her conquest. And in 'Christabel' likewise she has overpowered the Christian Self completely.

Again, in each case her power is exerted specifically over 'utterance'. The singing of the Abyssinian maid not only demonizes her listener, it inspires him to magical, paradise-building song. Freeing the Mariner from his dumbness, she frees his tongue only to tell the truth of her tale with 'strange power of speech' – which repeatedly takes possession of him, whether he likes it or not. Finally, her hypnotic, preternatural power controls Christabel's speech so utterly that the victim is like an otherwise dumb puppet of her will.

Geraldine is the ultimate incarnation of this power. And the whole action of 'Christabel' Part I, it could be said, is shaped to display the power in its moment of perfect triumph. Moreover, the power is convincingly authentic.* Geraldine declares the

* 'Christabel' Part II, which I will refer to here and there for convenience, simply makes this poem's relationship to 'The Ancient Mariner' more explicit. 'The Ancient Mariner' presented a portrait of the Mariner and the Nightmare Life-in-Death in a panoramic setting. As I described earlier, in 'Christabel' Part I Coleridge zooms into close-up, and reveals exactly what was going on between them. At this degree of magnification, the Mariner has separated into two people: Christabel (the ideal soul of his Christian Self) and her father,

omnipotence of her lordship over Christabel's utterance in what is both the climax of this poem (and therefore the climax of the entire Three Act Tragic Opera) and one of the most mesmeric incantations in English poetry:

> In the touch of this bosom there worketh a spell,
> Which is lord of thy utterance, Christabel!
> Thou knowest to-night, and wilt know to-morrow,
> This mark of my shame, this seal of my sorrow;
> > But vainly thou warrest,
> > > For this is alone in
> > Thy power to declare,
> > > That in the dim forest
> > Thou heard'st a low moaning,
> And found'st a bright lady, surpassingly fair . . .

The power of the music here masks the complexity of the very peculiar statement being made.

The search for the source of Coleridge's 'new principle' of metre, following the clues, as I have done here, into the symbolic system of his personal myth, seems to have led to this preternatural, weirdly composite female. Is it possible to identify her any more closely?

I have touched on her association with the Shaman's Goddess of Life and Death, Mother of the animals, with the Anath behind Jehovah, with Hel and Alphitos, with Isis and the Nightmare. But at bottom, Coleridge's sacred constants are the Oak, the Serpent in the Oak, and the Woman in the Oak. If acorns were apples, this would be the famous group in the garden of Eden. Apart from the familiar one in Genesis, mythic interpretations of this situation

---

'the aged knight, Sir Leoline' (his Christian Self's shell of moral and intellectual ego). The Nightmare Life-in-Death cried 'I've won!', and left the reader mystified. In 'Christabel' Parts I and II Coleridge presents the inside story, the full drama, behind that cry, and reveals just how the Serpent Woman overpowered the Mariner's susceptible soul as a first step to overpowering his moral and intellectual ego and thereby the whole man.

sometimes portray the Serpent and the Woman as two aspects of the one Goddess, or as the Goddess (the Serpent) and her High Priestess (the Woman). Sometimes there are two women, and the possible permutations multiply. The Serpent can then be the God, and the women the two opposed aspects of the Goddess. This last reality lies behind the myth of Adam's two consorts: Eve and the Demon Lilith and the Serpent's mysterious relationship to both, which cannot have been unknown to Coleridge. Listening more closely, with an ear to the body-language behind this mythic lexicon, one can't help hearing, in the 'mingled measure', the two voices of his mother and the voices he later divided between his two Saras. One imagines (almost sees!) the Oak and all its ramifications as a contorted hologram in his brain-scan, every word making it shiver like lightning. And when he prays, one imagines the Snake that wreathed and kissed his heart as a violent, rippling displacement in the downward spikes of his electrocardiograph. In other words, one feels the biological reality of a mythos that projected, on the cave-wall, in hallucinatory fashion, the drama of his nightmares, convulsed his behaviour, alienated his friends and dissolved his career. And though in another perspective it can be read as a large-scale, brilliantly concise, diagnostic, luminous vision of England's spiritual/intellectual predicament, it was a predicament that left Coleridge himself hanging on a cross.

In every perspective, Geraldine's rape of Christabel is the most powerful image of the nuclear event, the germinal event, in Coleridge's poetic life. This revelatory act is shocking on several counts, not only because a woman first hypnotizes then rapes a woman, or because she does it with such mysterious purpose (emerging from nowhere to do it). Since Geraldine is raping the 'soul' of Coleridge's Christian Self she is actually raping Coleridge too. She is simultaneously raping both the woman in the man and the man in the woman. Coleridge, as his verses make clear, is as overawed as Christabel by her erotic power and beauty. But what is truly shocking (unforgettable, unfathomable) is that this great beauty reveals, with a horrible deliberation, a bosom which is

70

('this mark of my shame, this seal of my sorrow') indescribably repulsive. The words that Coleridge uses (in Part II) to describe it, 'old', 'cold', and even the words he cancelled (from Part I), 'hideous, deformed and foul of hue', and 'A vision foul', are nothing to the horror of evil that he manages to suggest. Yet this 'mark of . . . shame' is the very proof of just who she is. And the fact that this being has not only revealed herself to him, but has taken possession of the 'soul' of his Christian Self, in this irreversible enforced abasement and act of possession, as the 'Lord' of the 'truth' of his utterance, is – for Coleridge – the 'truth impossible to face'.

Geraldine's 'human' nature in 'Christabel' establishes her centre of gravity, but what counts, for a reader, is her whole aura of suggestion, and that is the sum of her manifestations throughout the development of the visionary poems. Her corpse-like and reptilian bosom identifies the *divine* beauty (Coleridge uses the word to describe her eyes, which are the next moment 'shrunken serpent's eyes') as the 'greater than Jehovah'. Everything that has stirred in her history – the Fury Form of the 'great, nameless and malignant Female', the submarine giver of food and Mother of sea-creatures, the Abyssinian damsel with a dulcimer and the corpse-eating Nidhogg in Hel, the woman wailing in the chasm for her demon lover and the slimy things that crawled with legs in the rotting sea, the Nightingale and the love-maddened alligator, the Nightmare Life-in-Death and the Maenads that sent Ebon Ebon Thalud to tear out Coleridge's eyeball, Alphitos the leprous-faced night-goblin Goddess and the world-encircling serpent filling the sea with its luminous coils, the waning moon embracing a star and the wary, wily old long-breathed witch Nature, tough-lived as a turtle, Heaven's Mother, the Great Goddess of the putrefying, oceanic grave and the radiant cauldron of abounding new life, the river of erotic song and the sacred word: all these converged, with their metaphysical hinterworlds and dream-sargassos, into the coiled power of Geraldine. Like a Cleopatra-Cressida, from every 'joint and motive' of her paradoxical being she calls his Christian Self to surrender to her kind of love, the beauty of her truth and the fact of her lordship. This 'rape under hypnosis' is simply the ultimate form of her 'call'. It is the imperious seal of her possession, the *fait accompli*. And 'Christabel' Part I is her monumental poetic trophy, the final tableau of her triumphant will. At the close she reclines, satiated, like that snake wreathed around Coleridge's heart. And Christabel sleeps in her coils, helpless, violated and blissful.

Though it took some time for Coleridge to realize consciously what had happened, at bottom he understood instantly, and fled.

## XXIII Lord of Utterance

What Geraldine is actually saying, in that incantatory declaration of her will and omnipotence, is that though Christabel is now aware of Geraldine's loathsome secret – namely, her reptilian and corpselike *body* – nevertheless it is a secret she can never divulge. This comes as a hypnotic command, instructing her to speak of Geraldine henceforth only as 'surpassingly fair'. In the creaky Gothic plot this enforced secrecy has a creaky function. In Part II, Geraldine will move on to the next stage of her plan, seducing Christabel's father as easily as she has seduced Christabel, and Christabel must tell no tales.

But as the personification of the sacred Alph, the river of Coleridge's poetic word, she is saying something else – and saying it to Coleridge. Here it is not so much a hypnotic command as a statement of fact. Though his vision of her is one of terror, he will speak of her only as 'surpassingly fair'. Though he sees her as the Goddess of Death and the rotting sea, as well as the Goddess of Life and of the effulgent sea of birth, he will worship her as the wholly beautiful. That is to say, like Job he will glorify her beauty 'though it slay me'. This is not a poetic or religious perversity. It is a commonplace of the mystical life. Perhaps of the life of the dedicated scientist also. It is a simple recognition of the natural and presumably biological law that whatever is perceived as reality emits a compelling fascination indistinguishable from beauty. And this Female presented herself to Coleridge's unusual awareness as the ultimate reality, therefore the ultimate truth, therefore the ultimate beauty. The speech that expresses her reality, her truth, and so, inevitably (and as it were incidentally), her beauty, is therefore his 'sacred speech', his only genuine utterance.

That is how she comes to be sole 'lord' of his 'utterance'. And that is why his Christian Self, in its constant evasion of her and the dreadful life of her Oak Tree, has no sacred speech – only a Babel of intellectual tongues that plug Coleridge's ears from the 'call' of her truth, her reality, her beauty, and from any song out of the Oak.

When he rejects Geraldine and flees – he has renounced that speech. He is thereafter, from Geraldine's point of view, and from the point of view of his own 'sphere of acute feelings', speechless. However much he may talk and write, it is all non-language. Comparatively. His flight into Germany is therefore the third circle that he weaves around his Unleavened Self and Her.

This explains why his unique music is confined to so few poems: mainly the three visionary poems, with slight leakage into two or three others. It is confined to poems that deal with his myth – or rather with her myth. That core-like image cluster – woman/ reptile/oak – brings the clockwork inevitability of its meanings and dynamics with it wherever it appears, along with its distinctive 'sacred' language. But that is simply characteristic of the mythic poet. In Wordsworth's verse, the mythic elements are at once less distinctly formulated and more discursively diffused through a more unified temperament: the unique medicinal gum can exude at any moment, in the most unpromising corners. But in Coleridge's verse, unless this woman or her oak is about to appear, or is present, one finds only the exclusive wavelength and language of his Christian intellectual Self. Now and again these make an admirable poem – when they are braced against her painful absence, as a lament ('Dejection', 'Work Without Hope'), or are suffused by her nearness ('The Lime-Tree Bower', 'Frost at Midnight'). But such works are moulded of an utterly different stuff from the magical substance of the visionary poems, and Coleridge knew it, when he admitted to 'hating composition'. As the record proves, except for those few months of natural, blessed release, his efforts at 'composition' could find only the language of his Christian intellectual Self – the very language that denied him release.

But the myth could pick up unlikely masks – especially carnival masks. 'Fire, Famine and Slaughter' and 'The Devil's Thoughts' (which had the kind of impact on Byron and Shelley that 'The Knight's Tomb' had on Scott) give a hint of the Mephistophelian sprites that frisked around his Fairy Queen. Another *jeu d'esprit*, 'The Raven', in which one can feel a whole undeveloped oeuvre of inspired factotum doggerel (a huge loss), turns out to be centred solidly on the Oak. Apart from these, and one or two more muffled echoes, the only times we hear his Unleavened Self give voice are inadvertently and *sotto voce* in passages of his descriptive prose jottings, sketching the effects of light, leaves or water – where he slips through (tiptoes past his terrors) into a delicacy and impassioned *recitative* that has no equal before Hopkins.

But the most illuminating of these fragmentary glimpses into his myth is 'The Knight's Tomb'.


## XXIV On the Breast of Helvellyn

The Oak appears in 'The Knight's Tomb' – only to disappear. If 'The Raven' dramatizes the Unleavened Self's murderously vengeful rage over the demolition of the Oak, 'The Knight's Tomb' records Coleridge's mourning acceptance of the loss.

> Where is the grave of Sir Arthur O'Kellyn?
> Where may the grave of that good man be? –
> By the side of a spring, on the breast of Helvellyn,
> Under the twigs of a young birch tree!
> The oak that in summer was sweet to hear,
> And rustled its leaves in the fall of the year,
> And whistled and roared in the winter alone,
> Is gone, – and the birch in its stead is grown. –
> The Knight's bones are dust,

And his good sword rust; –
His soul is with the saints, I trust.

Here is another Paradise Mountain, a spring, and a tree. And under the tree something new – a dead man in his grave.

The Oak, that lived so sweetly and heroically through the seasons, has suddenly – without any explanation – gone. In its place, unqualified except by the quality-less adjective 'young', is a Birch tree.

The man died and the Oak tree went. The logic is: they were one and the same. Or, the life of the one was dependent on the life of the other. Now it has gone and he is under the ground that its boughs shaded. And over his buried corpse, in its place, is a Birch.

The name Sir Arthur O'Kellyn is one of those odd compounds invented by Coleridge, like Sir Henry, Lord Falkland, in 'The Ballad of the Dark Ladie', and the Baron Sir Leoline, Christabel's father, and Sir Roland de Vaux of Tryermaine, the father of Geraldine. According to his carefully assembled name, Sir Arthur was a Warrior (Knight), Celtic (O'Kellyn), and Royal Brythonic (Arthur). He was a warrior chieftain from the obscure front line of the Pagan/Christian deadlock – belonging in some fashion to both sides. Behind him, perhaps, opens the 'preternatural' dimension of the mythos of the Grail, the only realm in which integration of those two worlds might occur.

Within Coleridge's more particular, personal mythos, this figure (a form of Thor – Ar-Thur) is a Knight of the Oak. He is loosely related, therefore, to Sir Leoline, who fell so easily into the power of Geraldine, his daughter's seducer and usurper. Also to Sir Henry ('Ballad of the Dark Ladie') who was something of a Demon Lover. Also to the Mariner, whose quest was a modified 'Excursion of Thor' and none the less knightly for being made on shipboard rather than on horseback.

He is the half-noble negotiator between the two worlds, who lived in the possibility that the two might co-exist: a man of two selves. As if he might be a Coleridge who could suspend the prejudice of his Christian Self and give audience to his Unleavened Self – even to the point of becoming temporarily possessed by the Unleavened Self. The Coleridge who could, in a fascinated sort of way, allow the half-somnambulist (as if drugged) Christabel to be overpowered and seduced by the purposeful Geraldine (and could even, like Sir Leoline, himself succumb to Geraldine). The Coleridge who could, briefly, write the visionary poems as straight autobiography.

The fact that this person now lies in his grave, and that the Oak has gone, tells us that the negotiating faculty has died in Coleridge, who has accordingly retreated into exclusive self-identification with his Christian Self. He has thereby 'lost' his Unleavened Self – with its woman, its serpent, and its Oak. Nothing remains but the Christian Self, which is represented, as now appears, by the Birch. The Oak, that shared Sir Arthur's life, has been replaced by the Birch, over his grave.

But why on Helvellyn? Wordsworth's very own mountain, one might have thought. In every way, the poem is close to Christabel, but (by its subject) comes later. Though Coleridge would recite it, he did not publish it until he assembled his *Complete Poems* which came out the year of his death, in 1834. But some who knew him put its composition as early as 1802, two years after Wordsworth delivered the fatal blow. It commemorates Coleridge's own words, after all: 'The poet is dead in me.' But buried on Helvellyn. Why Helvellyn, Wordsworth's very threshold? Why not, as Sir Arthur might have preferred, Mount Abora? or some other mountain that could conceivably be a stand-in for Mount Abora?

But Helvellyn is just that. Coleridge's familiarity with the Norse Goddess of the Underworld could not have failed to prompt the association, during one of his regular walks across the top of this mountain, on his way from his own home in Keswick to Wordsworth's cottage in Grasmere and back. The mountain was sacred to all of them. Dorothy records how William, Coleridge and she had fantasized about building a house up there – a home for their poetic future. After the fateful three-day visit in October 1800 when Wordsworth, having raised Coleridge's hopes to the highest, with his first reception of the finished 'Christabel', suddenly reversed his opinion (perhaps not mincing his words, probably paraphrasing his lethal note about 'The Ancient Mariner' that Coleridge would not see till the volume was published), maybe Coleridge came back over Helvellyn. Whether he did or not, it would occur to him sooner or later, as the death-blow to his poetic hopes took effect, that the most fitting burial place would be the very site on which those hopes had dreamed of building their home. The mountain of Hel, no longer Hel the oracular Sybil but Hel the Goddess of death, was the appropriate grave-mound for the presiding poetic genius of the never-to-be-written 'Excursion of Thor'. Where he would lie in the coffin-ship of the Nightmare Life-in-Death herself. Moreover, it is likely enough that Coleridge had lit upon the Old Norse *vella*, to boil, and *vell*, a bubbling up, with their close links to old Scandinavian and English words for well-spring. That spring, beside which Sir Arthur lay, is in other words the fountain that boils up out of his Norse underworld from the roots of the great Tree. Closer than Mount Abora. The grimmer source within the 'mighty fountain' of the Alph.

But why was Thor's Oak replaced by a Birch tree? Why a Birch?

## xxv The White Birch and The Dark Ladie

Coleridge's many references to the Oak are countered, here and there, by his delight in the Birch. The airy, showering light of the silvery Birch is opposite, in obvious ways, to the Oak – and yet in his mythos, though it does not belong to that rooted 'strength' and truth of the heart's passions, it does offer a substitute happiness: the consoling pleasure of freedom from those passions: the promised pleasures of love not as it actually is, tragic and terrifying to him, but love as it ought to be – a nostalgia for an idealized love that might have been.

During the spring months in which he finished 'The Ancient Mariner' and composed Part I of 'Christabel', he was working on another 'Ballad' that was clearly striving to enter the same visionary freedom, intensity, depth – but failing. This was 'The Ballad of the Dark Ladie'.

Of this poem's narrative action Coleridge kept and published only a fragment – which has nevertheless an amputated kind of completeness. In one sense it is a code-book for the two long narratives, identifying the tight connections between them in simple terms.

It opens with the Dark Ladie weeping 'in silent pain' for her betrothed Knight to come to her 'over the hills'. This is a direct link to two of the five women in the three visionary poems: to the woman wailing for her demon lover in the holy chasm of the Alph's source, on the one hand, and to Christabel praying under the Oak for her lover 'that's far away'. These links become stronger as the poem develops.

The Dark Ladie is closer to the woman wailing for her demon lover in that she sits close to a brook that falls scattering down a rock face, and though not under a 'waning moon' she 'lingers' under a sun that is 'sloping down the sky' – towards the dark.

But she is closer to Christabel in that she is sitting on moss, under a tree. Though the tree above her is not the mistletoe-bunched, dragonish Oak, that brandished its many heads and tentacles over Christabel, but a Birch with 'silver bark', at least the moss from Christabel's Oak is here – beneath her. And it is the same moss, perhaps, that cushioned the knees of the Holy Hermit, in 'The Ancient Mariner', when he kneeled in prayer 'at morn, and noon, and eve', and that

> wholly hides
> The rotted old oak-stump.

As if the Holy Hermit, in spirit, might be there, with his invisible arm around her shoulder, and his protective voice in her ear. (It will turn out to be appropriate, too, that she seems to be sitting on Sir Arthur O'Kellyn's grave.)

According to these suggestions (from all three visionary poems), the Dark Ladie somehow incorporates the two women from the opposite ends of Coleridge's feminine spectrum: the pure-minded Christian virgin, like Christabel, and the reptilian siren from the abyss, like Geraldine. Everything about her that is silvery white expresses a Christabel, and everything about her that is dark conceals a Geraldine.

When her longed-for-knight comes over the hills, the stilted verses have prepared us for a stilted noble figure. But in the etymological tenacity of Coleridge's richly precise yet protean code of signs, that Griffin crest, the flying half-reptile, is ominous.

He turns out to be Lord Falkland. And even the homely Christian name Henry cannot quite domesticate the eponym – from the fringe of the Antarctic seas, the latitudes of the Albatross. The moment his name passes her lips:

> Lord Falkland, it is Thou!

the Dark Ladie reveals her own identity, and his, more nakedly:

> She springs, she clasps him round the neck.

This accidental-seeming hint of the Albatross floats on through her declaration:

> My Henry, I have given thee much,
> I gave what I can ne'er recall,
> I gave my heart, I gave my peace,
>     O Heaven! I gave thee all!

But it suddenly stiffens into solidity when having promised her the 'fairest' of his sire's 'Nine castles' (as if that might be the castle of the most desirable Muse) he suddenly asks her to:

> Wait only till the stars peep out . . .

> Wait only till the hand of eve
> Hath wholly closed yon western bars,
> And through the dark we two will steal
>     Beneath the twinkling stars!

The Dark Ladie's wavering oscillation between a Crucifix-pure Christabel and a love-sick woman inwardly wailing for her demon lover now goes hard over to Christabel Militant and sticks there. She recoils from his proposal with:

79

> The dark? the dark? No! not the dark?
> The twinkling stars? How, Henry? How?

The only excuse for this outburst is that she is talking in mythic algebra – using the signs made more explicit in 'The Ancient Mariner'. The 'dark' is the same that came in 'one stride' after the Nightmare Life-in-Death's winning throw and triumphant cry: 'I've won!' The stars are the same that rushed out, at the same moment. In that starry dark the waning moon will soon rise and she will find herself transmogrified, like the werewolf, to the woman wailing for her Demon Lover who is, as is now evident, Lord Falkland. Carrying on with the same algebraic system, she retorts:

> O God! 'twas in the eye of noon
> He pledged his sacred vow!
>
> And in the eye of noon my love
> Shall lead me from my mother's door,
> Sweet boys and girls all clothed in white
> Strewing flowers before:
>
> But first the nodding minstrels go . . .

This looks more and more like the Church Marriage Ceremony that went before the Feast – which the Mariner's spell-stopped listener found it impossible to join. And from which – burdened with the vision of the Goddess of rainbow sea-serpents and of the worms of the grave – he had to turn away. But the Dark Ladie goes brightly and blithely on with her wedding plans:

> With music meet for lordly bowers,
> The children next in snow-white vests.
> Strewing buds and flowers!
>
> And then my love and I shall pace,
> My jet black hair in pearly braids,
> Between our comely bachelors
> And blushing bridal maids.

In this evidently strained ritual (where Coleridge is struggling with the memory of his own forced marriage) the Christian Coleridge seems to be trying (speaking through the Dark Ladie) to persuade 'the betrothed knight' to do exactly as he did: remove the world of the Unleavened Self, embrace the Christian moral law. The Dark Ladie, in her Christabel persona, is certainly trying to persuade him.

Lord Falkland, one imagines, is listening in dismay. Hoping to embrace a Geraldine, he finds his neck locked in the arms of a Christabel. His dream of converting her into an Abyssinian singing girl and going wild to her instrument, perhaps on the Susquehanna where the alligators roar, seems to have walked straight into a trap. We can assume this because after his first love-call ('Come into the dark') he is struck dumb by her reaction, and never speaks another word.

Perhaps he is figuring desperately how he can wake up the recessive Geraldine and excite her to throw off the dominant and domineering Christabel. Or maybe the alternative is flitting through his head – a premature grave on Helvellyn.

The verse never breaks through into poetry and in fact it rehearses the ritual assassination of the poetic gift in Coleridge: a monologue asphyxiation by the Christian Self. It dramatizes, in other words, the utter suppression of Geraldine, the 'lord of utterance'. She appears in this poem only by reflection in Lord Falkland's confident expectation and summons, and in the Dark Ladie's darkness (in one note, Coleridge calls her The Black Ladie), which is concentrated passively in her 'jet black hair', where it will submit (without protest, according to Christabel) to the birch-silver 'pearly braids' of Christabel's bridal crown, and to the silver-whiteness that dresses every aspect of her wedding, and that is epitomized, at the opening of the poem, in the Birch Tree under which she sits.

The Birch Tree that has replaced the Oak on Sir Arthur's grave.

But, for a moment there in passing, the Dark Ladie Christabel was also the Albatross, heavy around Lord Falkland's neck.

Indeed, her whole oration about her perfect marriage is given while hanging around Lord Falkland's neck.

This is one of the clues to the place of the Albatross in the algebraic mythic system.

## xxvi The Interplay of the Three Planes

In the particular interpretation that I have followed, the single Tragic Opera of the three poems (and the two subsidiary poems) tells the autobiographical story of the conflict between Coleridge's two selves, as it was precipitated and brought to a climax by the reptilian Female's 'call'.

This autobiographical aspect of the Three-Act Drama constitutes one plane or level – what might be called the upper and dramatically active level – of the vision.

On that level, I interpreted the shift, in 'The Ancient Mariner', from the loathsome 'dead' Universe to the blessed 'living' Universe, as an effect of a sudden shift in the Mariner's outlook. I described it as a shift from the outlook of his Christian Self to that of his Unleavened Self. It has been described elsewhere as a shift from a new religion to an older religion – a 'regression' from narrowly Protestant Christian to archaic Pagan. Coleridge experiences his Pagan 'regression' as a breakthrough to a vision of greater spiritual meaning: his vision of the beauty of the sea-snakes, which renews his (the Mariner's) spiritual being, and redeems all the horrors of his Christian adventure. Nevertheless, when Coleridge's habitually dominant Christian attitude reasserts itself, after this brief, mystical reversal, the returned Mariner's experience is recounted, and heard, not as a vision of greater spiritual meaning, a revelation of the divine glory of the total creation, but as something unspeakably dreadful, incomprehensibly ominous and disheartening, a tale too terrible to be told or heard, like a curse.

And on the autobiographical level, that is how the vision did operate on Coleridge, like a curse – destroying his life.

It became a 'curse', however, only in so far as he rejected it –

only in so far as he refused the 'call'. The broken torso of Apollo commanded Rilke: 'You must change your life.' In Coleridge's case, to have accepted the vision and obeyed the 'call' would have meant renouncing Christianity (at least as completely as Goethe renounced it, re-adapting only what he needed to keep). What that conversion would have signified for Coleridge, simply in the way of social consequences, can be imagined. On the other hand, the traditional penalty for refusing the 'call' is death of some kind (which is why, in societies that observe such events closely, the 'call' itself is so much feared: no normal person wants either of the two options).

While the Three-Act Drama presents Coleridge's response to the 'call' on that autobiographical level, it also incorporates the archetypal, visionary world from which the 'call' emerges. This archetypal world constitutes a different, deeper level. Perhaps autobiographical factors gave it a distinctly Coleridgean aspect, or sensitized him to the particular form in which it revealed itself to him. At the same time it is clearly the same archetypal world that has revealed itself, in some not too dissimilar form, in all cultures, as one of the earliest, most profound, most intimately meaningful and all-embracing 'religious' truths. It is the world of the great Female of Life and Death, in whom the sexually irresistible 'bride' somehow embodies not only the animal and vegetable kingdoms, and the processes of the elements, but the extremes of the devouring grave and the maternal womb. These last two in particular, like her two selves fighting for dominance, do not so much alternate as coexist, each within the other.

On this deeper level, that shift from the loathsome 'dead' universe to the blessed 'living' universe, and from the leprous Aphrodite dicing with death to Mary Queen, Heaven's Mother, is not a shift from one religion to another. The whole vision exists firmly within a Pagan universe – a single universe. The shift is simply one pulse of the oscillation between those two extremes of the great Female's manifestation – a movement of the eyes with which her consort and son (the Mariner) encompasses her totality, in 'terror and adoration', as in Job.

The religious structure of that Pagan, archetypal level is therefore quite intact, beneath the equally intact structure of the Protestant (Jehovan) level. The theological implication of this comes clear if it is put slightly differently. As sketched out above, the negative pole of the Female's Universe has a different meaning on each level. On the deeper level, it is simply the dark half of her sacred completeness, a phase of her divinity. But on the upper level it is the disgusting and terrifying hell, which the Christian regards as evil and absolutely rejects. Likewise, the positive pole of the Female's Universe has a different meaning on each level, though less pronounced and not inverted – i.e. not contradictory or antithetical. On the upper level, if it can be accepted at all (and the subject of the poem, in one sense, is the difficulty of this acceptance), it is the benign Universe of Mary Queen, Heaven's Mother – that sole portion of the primitive, Pagan vision which one form of Christianity could assimilate. On the lower level it is the benign Universe of Mary Queen's historical predecessors, the same Goddess in non-Christian form, as it might be the benign Universe of a bountiful and forgiving Arnaquagssak.

This approach to full Pagan vision via something like Celtic Christian Catholicism, which the Protestant Mariner follows, casts light on Coleridge's occasional scattered remarks about Catholicism that qualify his usual severe reservations. It explains, maybe, why his Notebook pages about St Teresa suddenly blaze with a quite peculiar as if secretly infatuated intensity. As if his Christian Self, before it could surrender to the Serpentine Female (and all her works) in 'Christabel', had first to be immersed and softened in the Mariolatrous hyperaesthesia of 'The Ancient Mariner'.

In this way, his image of the upper Jehovan level and his image of the lower Pagan level are fused in a kind of pun. And the mechanism of this pun is not accidental or contrived, but true to historical reality.

What combines the two levels, in 'The Ancient Mariner', is a third level, which belongs to both: not so much a third level as a third plane, vertical to the horizontals of the other two and bisecting both. This is the shamanic plane, the plane along which the Mariner actually moves. Disabled by the conflict on the upper level, he is compelled to take to the shamanic plane and plunge himself in the healing wholeness of the lower level. In so far as he brings back the vision of that wholeness and the first-hand experience of living within it, he heals us too, which is one reason why we value 'The Ancient Mariner' as we do.

## xxvii Identikit of the Albatross

Wordsworth contributed the Albatross. Coleridge had played paranormal midwife for Wordsworth's creative psyche. Now Wordsworth proved that he could return the favour. He could smuggle at least one essential thing to Coleridge's awareness, out of Coleridge's hidden self, past Coleridge's self-censorship. But this is a common enough experience where two people share a wavelength of excitement.

So the white Albatross emerged from the Alph's nest of images – as it might be the Alphatross. And however we look at it, the bird's rightness is uncanny.

In the most general sense, the Albatross in flight, and in friendly attendance on the ship, is the bird form of the 'call' – and as I mentioned earlier is therefore the bird-form of the great Female (like Vuokho), or in this case of the Nightmare Life-in-Death.

When the Mariner shoots it, the act is the Christian Self's declaration of war against the Unleavened Self and against the archetypal plane of the great Female which it represents.

At the same time, on the shamanic plane the bird is that Keeper of The Threshold – the animal form whose sacrificial death opens the spiritual vision.

But the more intricate meanings of the Albatross emerge most clearly with the help of 'The Ballad of the Dark Ladie', if the Albatross is regarded as the Dark Ladie herself. In this perspective, the significance of the Albatross is tightly linked to the plane of the autobiographical conflict.

The bird contains both of the Dark Ladie's selves – the Christabel Christian Self and the Geraldine Unleavened Self.

As it flies, and plays about the ship, it is the Dark Ladie *Geraldine*, wailing or weeping 'in silent pain' for her lover (in other words, uttering the 'call'). But as the bolt from the Mariner's Crucifix Crossbow penetrates it, the Geraldine spirit – i.e. the bird's *life* – is killed in it.

The falling bird then changes in mid-air. The dead Albatross that hits the deck is the living Dark Ladie *Christabel* – i.e. the bird's *death* – stepping to her wedding, or at least insisting that the ceremony be 'white' and 'in the eye of noon'.

The Mariner has made his conscious decision to refuse the 'call'. He must now be taught how he has unconsciously made the opposite decision, and has, by that very killing surrendered to the 'call'. The Mariner has murdered the Albatross in his Christian life of the 'lie'. He will now be taught what that means in the Unleavened life of the 'truth', where what he thought was a murder is in fact a sacrifice.

The Female, who is all the elements and creatures of the wind and sea, sweeps him to the confrontation and judgement.

The process of judgement, punishment and correction begins in the 'silent sea', as a paralysis of Heaven and Earth. The water of feeling and of heartfelt utterance – the water of Alph, no less – is as if dried up, even though the ship sits on an ocean of it. Language itself dries up – the language of the Christian Self, that is (the prayer to Jehovah), and the tongue withers. The water, which should be life, now appears to be death, and actually rots.

This is how the great Female's universe appears to the Christian Self who could not accept it. The Christian Crossbow Self not only rejected it, but, by killing its messenger the Albatross, killed it too.

The Christian Crossbow Self has performed the role of 'a Death' – dealing apparent death.

Considering the situation as a game, one could say the Christian Crossbow Self has won the first round, and in winning has forced on to the bird and the sea of the Female (the waters of Alph) a state like death, and on to itself a life of horror, dumbly staring at the world of its own death-dealing rejection, a world that seems to putrefy.

At which point the Mariner finds the Albatross hanging round his neck.

In the general sense, the Albatross is now two things. It is the Mariner's Christian Crossbow Self, with its burden of 'agony', its 'cross', which is the consequence of being Coleridge's Christian self. And at the same time it is the Christian Self's victim – the dead emanation of the 'lifeless ocean' of the rejected great Female's 'call'.

But in the more particular and precise sense, the Albatross hanging around the Mariner's neck is identical to the Dark Ladie Christabel hanging around the neck of Lord Falkland in 'The Ballad of the Dark Ladie'.

In that poem, Christabel triumphs in the end. At Lord Falkland's mention of the 'dark' and the 'stars', she assumes total defensive possession of the Dark Ladie's body. Her monologue insistence on a birch-white wedding in 'the eye of noon' is like a two-way exorcism. As if while with her left arm she hung around Lord Falkland's neck, with her right hand she lifted the pearly crucifix from between her breasts and held it up between their mouths, interdicting his lustful kiss and simultaneously banishing the demon lover/Unleavened Self from him and the spirit of Geraldine from herself.

As I noted, Falkland stands dumb, as if his tongue were 'withered at the root', and the displaced Geraldine slumps inside Christabel like a dead bird. Dark Ladie Christabel hangs on Lord Falkland's neck, that is, like the death-dealing Crucifix Crossbow combined with the murdered Albatross: 'a Death' carrying its winnings.

In the unsuccessful, aborted 'Ballad of the Dark Ladie', the game ends there, with the Dark Ladie Christabel still a clear winner and Lord Falkland staring over her shoulder at the death of his world of Eros. Just as the Mariner stares over the shoulders of the dead Albatross at the putrefying sea. Just as Coleridge stared over the shoulders of his colder and colder wife he wanted to love but could not.

The pivotal event of 'The Ancient Mariner' is the Mariner's transformation from the Protestant Christian who cannot pray in his world of loathsome death, to the (quasi-Catholic) Pagan spontaneously blessing the Creation in his world of radiant life. This sudden overthrow of the Christian Self by the Unleavened Self can be followed as the overthrow of the Christabel Self by the suddenly reviving Geraldine Self within the Dark Ladie form of the Albatross.

The overthrow could not happen in 'The Ballad of the Dark Ladie', much as Lord Falkland wanted it to, but in 'The Ancient Mariner' it can and does. The game here is far from over. When the Mariner sees the dark bars fleck the setting sun, Geraldine comes awake in the body of the Albatross. When the Mariner bites his arm, she returns irresistibly to life (and the Mariner is able to speak).

The opposition of these two female players, and the state of play, within the Dark Ladie Albatross, is now projected into the 'spectre bark' – the Christabel Christian Self being represented by 'a Death' and the Unleavened Geraldine Self by a lunar, deathly, beautiful woman. And now it turns out that the Dark Ladie Christabel's winning throw was illusory, and her gains temporary. The blood-drinking, supernatural Female, coming fully to life, makes the winning throw that concludes the game. Her cry: 'I've won!' means 'It is all mine!' – i.e. Coleridge and the Universe. At once, the partial outlook of the 'lie' begins to fail and the revelation of the all-inclusive 'truth' to take over.

This transformation is also projected – on to the Christian crew, who now drop dead, and on to the heavens, where the 'dark' arrives, the stars 'rush out', and the waning moon rises. Gradually the curse in the eyes of the dead Christian crew – more terrible and damning than an orphan's curse – shrivels away (as in the eyes of the Dark Ladie Christabel, perhaps, as she still clings around Lord Falkland's neck), and gives place to the radiance of the moonlit sea, full of beautiful sea-creatures, teeming with holy life. As if Lord Falkland were to find, instead of censorious Christabel,

Geraldine brilliantly alive in his arms, kissing him in the 'deep, romantic chasm', under the suddenly risen moon. Now that the sea-Female has absolutely won, and has returned to full possession of her own creation, the Mariner (part of her winnings) blesses what he sees in a rapture of recognition. At that point the Albatross, like the last vestige of his lethal Crossbow Christian Self, and the last weight of the now truly dead Dark Ladie Christabel, drops from his neck into the sea.

But again, one imagines the bird's mid-air falling corpse changing as before but in the opposite direction, and returning to what it was, to its true Geraldine-like life – if not to a living Albatross then to a sea-serpent of splendour and fluorescence, that plunges under and swirls away in flaring rainbow glories, among all the rejoicing sea-snakes.

Over this scene the waning moon with its star 'within the nether tip' lifts the Goddess's archaic banner. The Mariner is the star. And Coleridge himself is up there, in the lap of the 'great, malignant, nameless Female' (the one young STC ran out into the 'dreadful, stormy night' to find), now more blessed than Heaven's Mother, and in fact he climbs through the abyss with her in a rapturous embrace.*

* Remembering Pantisocracy's paradisal dream of life on the Susquehanna, in the American South, and drifting south still further, Coleridge might have recognized the tragic departure, on a raft of snakes, of the Mexican Redeemer god, Quetzalcoatl. After his intoxicated surrender to Xochiquetzal (the Aztec Anatha), Quetzalcoatl rose to become the morning star (the star near the waning moon). Then instead of composing 'The Knight's Tomb', as elegy for his poetic genius, Coleridge might have transcribed Quetzalcoatl's own lament for himself:

> He made a lament, a song
> About his going. He sang:
> 'Our Mother
> The Goddess with her mantle of serpents
> Is taking me with her
> As her child.
> I weep.'

Briefly. And only in these poems. Before he wakes up to what has happened.

## Postscript: The Snake in the Spine

The stark either/or of Coleridge's Christian dilemma, in the three visionary poems, came partly from the fact that his 'other God', the god of the alternative truth, the 'greater than Jehovah', took the form which in all orthodox Christian contexts is the very incarnation of Evil: the Snake.

The irruptive, 'preternatural' element of his revelatory experience could have conceivably taken on several different forms, any of which might have served as a workable expressive image. And one can't help wondering whether he wouldn't have found things easier, and his main problem more soluble, if only he had settled on a more evolved, less notoriously proscribed, less exacting symbol than the Snake – in the way that (confronting a conflict of broadly similar forces) Shakespeare and Eliot did.

One thing that cannot be doubted about Coleridge is the hundred per cent authenticity of his instinctive high-minded 'goodness'. His inborn benevolence of heart, spirit and mind was, in its way, a passion that determined all his other passions. It can often be felt directly, almost as a selflessness, almost, at times, as a latent saintliness. It can be felt in the poems as pervasively as in the Notebooks – in his exalted absorption with the sea-snakes and with Geraldine's uncanny beauty as unmistakably as in his persistent, costly humility of love towards his 'cruel' friends. It emanates convincingly from the whole man, not just from the vigilant piety of his Christian Self. Indeed, his Christian Self's narrow absolutism, occasionally sharpened to sectarian petulance (against Catholicism, for instance) by what he himself recognized, and regretted, as an intellectual vehemence that could resemble arrogance, was what most often displaced and obscured it. At the same time, it was most nakedly displayed in the poetry of his most intense visionary moments. Perhaps for many readers, this is still the paradox of the poems and of Coleridge the Christian moralist:

the fact that the 'evil' (in 'The Ancient Mariner' the sea-reptiles, in 'Christabel' Geraldine's serpent self) is the bearer of the omnipotent 'preternatural' beauty – which transfigures in the first poem the Mariner and in the second Christabel herself. Or, to put it another way, while that mystical love of goodness pervaded his whole nature, yet his poems revealed, and in a sense proved, that for him it radiated, as from a nucleus, from what his Church held to be the very symbol of evil.

In the poems the Serpent is assimilated to the Woman. A post-Freudian could well give this Woman of Coleridge's a role that is in the circumstances just as negative, from the post-Freudian point of view, as the Serpent is from the Christian. That is to say, the demonized lover/singer of 'Kubla Khan', with 'his flashing eyes, his floating hair', could be suspected of having drunk the milk and honey-dew not of Paradise but simply of the womb.

Just so, in 'The Ancient Mariner', after the collapse of his Christian vision of the woman's ocean as a waterless hell of death, the Mariner suddenly accepts it as a dazzling paradise of love, and falls into a trance of sleep while his whole body drinks in bliss in the rocking womb or cradle of the ship. Again, Christabel the same, when she wakes ravished – wholly possessed – in the wreathing arms of Geraldine:

> O sorrow and shame! Can this be she,
> The lady, who knelt at the old oak tree?
> And lo! the worker of these harms,
> That holds the maiden in her arms,
> Seems to slumber still and mild,
> As a mother with her child.
>
> A star hath set, a star hath risen,
> O Geraldine! since arms of thine
> Have been the lovely lady's prison.
> O Geraldine! one hour was thine –
> Thou'st had thy will! By tairn and rill,
> The night-birds all that hour were still.
> But now they are jubilant anew,

> From cliff and tower, tu-whoo! tu-whoo!
> Tu-whoo! tu-whoo! from wood and fell!
>
> And see! the lady Christabel
> Gathers herself from out her trance;
> Her limbs relax, her countenance
> Grows sad and soft; the smooth thin lids
> Close o'er her eyes; and tears she sheds –
> Large tears that leave the lashes bright!
> And oft the while she seems to smile
> As infants at a sudden light!

Looked at in this way, the Snake Woman appears not only as the personification of the delusory, as-if-almighty glamour of evil, she can also be seen as a symptom of infantilism in Coleridge.

A defender of Coleridge has to shift everything into an altogether bigger arena, and to find a better word than the psychoanalyst's disparaging *infantilism*. Coleridge himself considered a certain child-heartedness to be an adult's highest human endowment. He derived this not from the spiritual and wisdom traditions of China and India, where it is a basic tenet, but from his own perception. He links it specifically with the physiology of language:

> To trace the if not absolute birth yet the growth and endurance of Language from the Mother talking to the child at her Breast –
>
> (Notebook)

and with unspoiled consciousness:

> To carry on the feelings of childhood into the powers of manhood, to combine the child's sense of wonder and novelty with the familiar . . . , this is the character and priviledge of genius, and one of the marks which distinguish genius from talents.
>
> (Essay xv, 'The Friend')

But his more esoteric blissful sense of the 'preternatural' Woman who is also a Serpent hearkens further back still, beyond his childhood and mother's womb.

In Pagan religions the Snake is almost without exception a positive figure, anything but evil, though sometimes 'terrible' – and often the highest deity.

Perhaps this seems to suggest that beneath his efforts to be a pure, whole-hearted Christian, Coleridge was in fact a pure, whole-hearted, genuine Pagan, something like the regenerate Apuleius at the end of *The Golden Ass*. But things were obviously not so simple. Or perhaps they were much simpler. His attitude to the Serpent Woman had nothing fanciful about it, nothing nostalgic, no archaicizing in the bad sense. It was first hand, existential, peremptory, overwhelming and incomprehensible to him. In that case, one has to consider what might seem unlikely.

The Serpent and the Woman combined appear again, beyond 'paganism', in the spiritual asceticism of India. Fundamental to all forms of yoga is the ideal purpose of awakening *Kundalini*. In the curious biological apperception of Indian spirituality, this is 'the serpent power' that successful yogic practice awakens at the base of the spine and raises up, through the body, from station to station, via the spine, eventually to the crown of the head. As it ascends, this elemental, thaumaturgic energy awakens each successive centre of 'preternatural' faculties – culminating in a transfigured state of illumination regarded as union with the True Self, the highest 'divine' condition of Being attainable to human consciousness. The vast literature of Indian spirituality revolves around this first practical essential: the awakening of the dormant spinal power. When it does awaken, it is experienced in vision as a Serpent, and is always described as a Serpent, except when it is experienced and described as the 'Divine Mother'.

The 'awakening' of the serpent power is not confined to practising yogis. It may awaken of itself, to some degree, in any person of passionately concentrated inner life – as in the often experienced paranormal episodes that accompany intense love, or that may develop out of a suffering that is inescapable, acute and

prolonged enough. According to the anecdotal biographic litera-
ture, wherever the person is unprepared (by the necessary
psychic and physical training and guidance) the psychosomatic
effects of the Serpent's ascent can be chaotic, terrifying, seemingly
pathological, and may last for years. If opium and his struggle
against it were not confusing the picture, Coleridge's extra-
ordinary physical symptoms might well qualify. Even so, no
matter what the external life, the serpent power becomes the
bringer (the Mother), eventually, of some portion of spiritual gifts
(healing powers etc.) if not of the ultimate illumination. There is a
parallel to the sophisticated, assiduously cultivated Indian pheno-
menon, as well as to the rough and ready commonplace, sponta-
neous one, in the experiences and arduous training initiations that
produce traditional Shamans, the *Angekoks*.

Setting Coleridge's vision in this *biological** context, one
wonders whether it could have been induced by a spiritual
awakening of that kind – spontaneously undergone by his
*Unleavened Self*. The abnormal intensity and 'authority' of the
vision suggests the possibility. His account of it, which engaged
him in such moral struggle, could then be seen as the result of an
over-crystallization of the imagery and an over-literal interpret-
ation of it in Christian terms. That would be inevitable from his
Christian Self's point of view. In other words – historically
deprived of any adequate symbolic (mythic) paradigms and
conceptual categories, such as might represent the reality of that
experience, his Protestant Christianity would mistranslate it,
automatically, as evil Snake business. His artistic problem
became: how can the revelation be expressed through a language
of signs in which it can appear only as the opposite of itself? As the
poems show, he solved the problem by shifting to another

* 'Biological' in the sense that 'the serpent power' can be regarded as a
usually dormant resource, the most primordial, fundamental,
emergency resource, of our animal body, one that has, when aroused,
seemingly supernatural, centralizing, unifying, intensifying effects on
developed consciousness.

language. He relaxed from the Protestant language in which the poems are framed, and thence dissolved through a Catholic into a wholly Pagan language in the core of the vision presented. Supposing, as I say, that the Serpent Power was his true subject, the Pagan mythos simply became his appropriate symbol of it.

If this supposition were true, if in his case the Serpent Power truly had awakened and moved, it would help to explain the apparent inconsistency: the coexistence, in him, of his benevolent, spiritualized potentially saintly passion of passions, and of the peculiar yet transcendent Snake and Snake Woman imagery in the great poems.

There is an Indian tradition that Christ spent his lost seventeen years in the Himalayas, among Kashmiri yogic adepts. His mountain-top shrine is famous and still venerated. If that had been likewise an accepted Western tradition, known to Coleridge in all its circumstances (and as likely as any other), as it is to us now, we might find it easier to set the radical, primitive, extra-Christian inclusiveness of his religous feeling in a positive context. And easier to grant a positive value to what he glimpsed of the Snake and the Woman – on the far side of his Christian Self's busy ratiocinations. We might then be able to say: what opposed and challenged his defensive, orthodox Christianity was not so much an 'Unleavened Self' as a greater holistic revelation, more truly like Christ's own, more self-evidently that of a greater 'god of love'.


One imagines Coleridge's own mythos emanating from three octaves: the higher 'preternatural' octave, the middle Pagan octave, the lower womb-world octave. In the higher octave, the Kundalini power ascending resonates 'divine' illuminations, the authority and actual presence of the 'divine', from the images of the Snake and the Great Female. In the middle octave, the 'song' of the Pagan double-natured Serpent Woman of Sexuality and death 'translates', incorporates and transmits the revelation and real power of the higher octave. In the lower octave, the 'symphony' of the earth-enfolding Serpent and Mother-womb accompanies in contrapuntal harmony and with rich chordal effects the 'song' of the middle octave. All three octaves are centred on the spinal 'tree' through which Kundalini climbs. In mythic narrative terms, Kundalini attempts to wholly take possession of Coleridge and so to transform him, which becomes the drama of 'the call'. His awareness of that produced the spontaneous musical vision for which he laboured to find the metrical/rhythmical expression.

It is in this sense that in rejecting 'the call', his Christian Self rejected the 'greater god'. Or rather, in this sense his Christian Self censored everything but a generalized mystical passion for 'goodness' and an incandescent religiosity – which remained as the staples of his existence.

These crumbs from the supper of the Great Snake and the Serpent Woman were all that he could bring into his daily life. Except for that brief period, when he returned with the three poems.

## Note

While my remarks in this essay are based mainly on easily accessible material in Coleridge's Poems and Notebooks, Coleridge biography, J. L. Lowes's *Road to Xanadu*, and common knowledge about such things as Norse myth, the King James Bible, the ballads, etc., I do draw heavily on two other sources that may be unfamiliar to many students of English poetry.

One of these is the history of the cult of the Female in religious tradition. In particular, I draw on one view of this history, in which it can be seen to illuminate aspects of mankind's psychological evolution – both as this evolution has been experienced (and expressed) in the long development of recorded human cultures, and as it is recapitulated (sometimes, as in Coleridge, with great self-awareness) in the psycho-biological life of individuals. For curious readers, a graphic overview of the vast lineaments of the subject can be found in Erich Neumann's *The Origins and History of*

*Consciousness* (translated by R. F. C. Hull, Princeton/Bollingen, 1954) and *The Great Mother: An Analysis of the Archetype* (translated by Ralph Mannheim, Princeton/Bollingen, 1955) – especially in the latter. A more detailed account of the material itself is supplied by *The Myth of the Goddess*, by Anne Baring and Jules Cashford (Viking, 1991).

The other source to which I owe a good deal is the literature dealing with shamanism. The unchanging spontaneity and ubiquity of shamanic experience, its place in the history of both great and small artistic and spiritual traditions, and its direct connection with the manner and subject matter of certain kinds of poetry, is well worth looking into. The best-known introduction to the phenomenon is Mircea Eliade's *Shamanism: Archaic Techniques of Ecstasy* (translated by Willard Trask, London: Routledge, 1964).

A CHOICE OF COLERIDGE'S VERSE

# The Raven

## A Christmas Tale Told by a School-boy to his Little Brothers and Sisters

Underneath an old oak tree
There was of swine a huge company,
That grunted as they crunched the mast:
For that was ripe, and fell full fast.
Then they trotted away, for the wind grew high:
One acorn they left, and no more might you spy.
Next came a Raven, that liked not such folly:
He belonged, they did say, to the witch Melancholy!
Blacker was he than blackest jet,
Flew low in the rain, and his feathers not wet.
He picked up the acorn and buried it straight
By the side of a river both deep and great.

      Where then did the Raven go?
      He went high and low,
Over hill, over dale, did the black Raven go.
      Many Autumns, many Springs
      Travelled he with wandering wings:
      Many Summers, many Winters –
      I can't tell half his adventures.

At length he came back, and with him a She,
And the acorn was grown to a tall oak tree.
They built them a nest in the topmost bough,
And young ones they had, and were happy enow.
But soon came a Woodman in leathern guise,
His brow, like a pent-house, hung over his eyes.
He'd an axe in his hand, not a word he spoke,
But with many a hem! and a sturdy stroke,
At length he brought down the poor Raven's own oak.
His young ones were killed; for they could not depart,
And their mother did die of a broken heart.

The boughs from the trunk the Woodman did sever;
And they floated it down on the course of the river.
They sawed it in planks, and its bark they did strip,
And with this tree and others they made a good ship.
The ship, it was launched; but in sight of the land
Such a storm there did rise as no ship could withstand.
It bulged on a rock, and the waves rush'd in fast:
Round and round flew the Raven, and cawed to the blast.
He heard the last shriek of the perishing souls –
See! see! o'er the topmast the mad water rolls!

    Right glad was the Raven, and off he went fleet,
And Death riding home on a cloud he did meet,
And he thank'd him again and again for this treat:

    They had taken his all, and REVENGE IT WAS SWEET!

# Frost at Midnight

The Frost performs its secret ministry,
Unhelped by any wind. The owlet's cry
Came loud – and hark, again! loud as before.
The inmates of my cottage, all at rest,
Have left me to that solitude, which suits
Abstruser musings: save that at my side
My cradled infant slumbers peacefully.
'Tis calm indeed! so calm, that it disturbs
And vexes meditation with its strange
And extreme silentness. Sea, hill, and wood,
This populous village! Sea, and hill, and wood,
With all the numberless goings on of life,
Inaudible as dreams! the thin blue flame
Lies on my low burnt fire, and quivers not;
Only that film, which fluttered on the grate,
Still flutters there, the sole unquiet thing.
Methinks, its motion in this hush of nature
Gives it dim sympathies with me who live,
Making it a companionable form,
Whose puny flaps and freaks the idling Spirit
By its own moods interprets, every where
Echo or mirror seeking of itself,
And makes a toy of Thought.

                But O! how oft,
How oft, at school, with most believing mind,
Presageful, have I gazed upon the bars,
To watch that fluttering *stranger*! and as oft
With unclosed lids, already had I dreamt
Of my sweet birth-place, and the old church-tower,
Whose bells, the poor man's only music, rang
From morn to evening, all the hot Fair-day,
So sweetly, that they stirred and haunted me

With a wild pleasure, falling on mine ear
Most like articulate sounds of things to come!
So gazed I, till the soothing things I dreamt
Lulled me to sleep, and sleep prolonged my dreams!
And so I brooded all the following morn,
Awed by the stern preceptor's face, mine eye
Fixed with mock study on my swimming book:
Save if the door half opened, and I snatched
A hasty glance, and still my heart leaped up,
For still I hoped to see the *stranger*'s face,
Townsman, or aunt, or sister more beloved,
My play-mate when we both were clothed alike!

Dear Babe, that sleepest cradled by my side,
Whose gentle breathings, heard in this deep calm,
Fill up the interspersed vacancies
And momentary pauses of the thought!
My babe so beautiful! it thrills my heart
With tender gladness, thus to look at thee,
And think that thou shalt learn far other lore
And in far other scenes! For I was reared
In the great city, pent 'mid cloisters dim,
And saw nought lovely but the sky and stars.
But thou, my babe! shalt wander like a breeze
By lakes and sandy shores, beneath the crags
Of ancient mountain, and beneath the clouds,
Which image in their bulk both lakes and shores
And mountain crags: so shalt thou see and hear
The lovely shapes and sounds intelligible
Of that eternal language, which thy God
Utters, who from eternity doth teach
Himself in all, and all things in himself.
Great universal Teacher! he shall mould
Thy spirit, and by giving make it ask.

Therefore all seasons shall be sweet to thee,
Whether the summer clothe the general earth

With greenness, or the redbreast sit and sing
Betwixt the tufts of snow on the bare branch
Of mossy apple-tree, while the nigh thatch
Smokes in the sun-thaw; whether the eave-drops fall
Heard only in the trances of the blast,
Or if the secret ministry of frost
Shall hang them up in silent icicles,
Quietly shining to the quiet Moon.

# This Lime-Tree Bower My Prison

Well, they are gone, and here must I remain,
This lime-tree bower my prison! I have lost
Beauties and feelings, such as would have been
Most sweet to my remembrance even when age
Had dimmed mine eyes to blindness! They, meanwhile,
Friends, whom I never more may meet again,
On springy heath, along the hill-top edge,
Wander in gladness, and wind down, perchance,
To that still roaring dell, of which I told;
The roaring dell, o'erwooded, narrow, deep,
And only speckled by the mid-day sun;
Where its slim trunk the ash from rock to rock
Flings arching like a bridge – that branchless ash,
Unsunn'd and damp, whose few poor yellow leaves
Ne'er tremble in the gale, yet tremble still,
Fanned by the water-fall! and there my friends
Behold the dark green file of long lank weeds,
That all at once (a most fantastic sight!)
Still nod and drip beneath the dripping edge
Of the blue clay-stone.

             Now, my friends emerge
Beneath the wide wide Heaven – and view again
The many-steepled tract magnificent
Of hilly fields and meadows, and the sea,
With some fair bark, perhaps, whose sails light up
The slip of smooth clear blue betwixt two Isles
Of purple shadow! Yes! they wander on
In gladness all; but thou, methinks, most glad,
My gentle-hearted Charles! for thou hast pined
And hungered after Nature, many a year,
In the great City pent, winning thy way
With sad yet patient soul, through evil and pain

And strange calamity! Ah! slowly sink
Behind the western ridge, thou glorious Sun!
Shine in the slant beams of the sinking orb,
Ye purple heath-flowers! richlier burn, ye clouds!
Live in the yellow light, ye distant groves!
And kindle, thou blue Ocean! So my friend
Struck with deep joy may stand, as I have stood,
Silent with swimming sense; yea, gazing round
On the wide landscape, gaze till all doth seem
Less gross than bodily; and of such hues
As veil the Almighty Spirit, when yet he makes
Spirits perceive his presence.

                    A delight
Comes sudden on my heart, and I am glad
As I myself were there! Nor in this bower,
This little lime-tree bower, have I not mark'd
Much that has sooth'd me. Pale beneath the blaze
Hung the transparent foliage; and I watch'd
Some broad and sunny leaf, and lov'd to see
The shadow of the leaf and stem above
Dappling its sunshine! And that walnut-tree
Was richly ting'd, and a deep radiance lay
Full on the ancient ivy, which usurps
Those fronting elms, and now, with blackest mass
Makes their dark branches gleam a lighter hue
Through the late twilight: and though now the bat
Wheels silent by, and not a swallow twitters,
Yet still the solitary humble-bee
Sings in the bean-flower! Henceforth I shall know
That Nature ne'er deserts the wise and pure;
No plot so narrow, be but Nature there,
No waste so vacant, but may well employ
Each faculty of sense, and keep the heart
Awake to Love and Beauty! and sometimes
'Tis well to be bereft of promis'd good,

That we may lift the soul, and contemplate
With lively joy the joys we cannot share.
My gentle-hearted Charles! when the last rook
Beat its straight path along the dusky air
Homewards, I blest it! deeming, its black wing
(Now a dim speck, now vanishing in light)
Had cross'd the mighty Orb's dilated glory,
While thou stood'st gazing; or when all was still,
Flew creeking o'er thy head, and had a charm
For thee, my gentle-hearted Charles, to whom
No sound is dissonant which tells of Life.

# The Wanderings of Cain
## Prefatory Note

A prose composition, one not in metre at least, seems *prima facie* to require explanation or apology. It was written in the year 1798, near Nether Stowey, in Somersetshire, at which place (*sanctum et amabile nomen* [holy and beloved name]! rich by so many associations and recollections) the author had taken up his residence in order to enjoy the society and close neighbourhood of a dear and honoured friend, T. Poole, Esq. The work was to have been written in concert with another [Wordsworth], whose name is too venerable within the precincts of genius to be unnecessarily brought into connection with such a trifle, and who was then residing at a small distance from Nether Stowey. The title and subject were suggested by myself, who likewise drew out the scheme and the contents for each of the three books or cantos, of which the work was to consist, and which, the reader is to be informed, was to have been finished in one night! My partner undertook the first canto: I the second: and which ever had *done first*, was to set about the third. Almost thirty years have passed by; yet at this moment I cannot without something more than a smile moot the question which of the two things was the more impracticable, for a mind so eminently original to compose another man's thoughts and fancies, or for a taste so austerely pure and simple to imitate the Death of Abel? Methinks I see his grand and noble countenance as at the moment when having despatched my own portion of the task at full finger-speed, I hastened to him with my manuscript – that look of humorous despondency fixed on his almost blank sheet of paper, and then its silent mock-piteous admission of failure struggling with the sense of the exceeding ridiculousness of the whole scheme – which broke up in a laugh: and the Ancient Mariner was written instead.

Years afterward, however, the draft of the plan and proposed incidents, and the portion executed, obtained favour in the eyes of more than one person, whose judgment on a poetic work could not but have weighed with me, even though no parental partiality had been thrown into the same scale, as a make-weight: and I determined on commencing anew, and composing the whole in stanzas, and made some progress in realising this intention, when adverse gales drove my bark off the 'Fortunate Isles' of the Muses: and then other and more momentous interests prompted a different voyage, to firmer anchorage and a securer port. I have in vain tried to recover the lines from the palimpsest tablet of my memory: and I can only offer the introductory stanza, which had been committed to writing for the purpose of procuring a friend's judgment on the metre, as a specimen: –

Encinctured with a twine of leaves,
That leafy twine his only dress!
A lovely Boy was plucking fruits,
By moonlight, in a wilderness.
The moon was bright, the air was free,
And fruits and flowers together grew
On many a shrub and many a tree:
And all put on a gentle hue,
Hanging in the shadowy air
Like a picture rich and rare.
It was a climate where, they say,
The night is more belov'd than day.
But who that beauteous Boy beguil'd,
That beauteous Boy to linger here?
Alone, by night, a little child,
In place so silent and so wild –
Has he no friend, no loving mother near?

I have here given the birth, parentage, and premature decease of the 'Wanderings of Cain, a poem', – intreating, however, my Readers, not to think so meanly of my judgment as to suppose that I either regard or offer it as any excuse for the publication of the following fragment (and I may add, of one or two others in its neighbourhood) in its primitive crudity. But I should find still greater difficulty in forgiving myself were I to record pro *taedio* publico [for public *boredom*] a set of petty mishaps and annoyances which I myself wish to forget. I must be content therefore with assuring the friendly Reader, that the less he attributes its appearance to the Author's will, choice, or judgment, the nearer to the truth he will be.

S. T. Coleridge (1828)


CANTO II

'A little further, O my father, yet a little further, and we shall come into the open moonlight.' Their road was through a forest of fir-trees; at its entrance the trees stood at distances from each other, and the path was broad, and the moonlight and the moonlight shadows reposed upon it, and appeared quietly to inhabit that solitude. But soon the path winded and became narrow, the sun at high noon sometimes speckled, but never illuminated it, and now it was dark as a cavern.

'It is dark, O my father!' said Enos, 'but the path under our feet is smooth and soft, and we shall soon come out into the open moonlight.'

'Lead on, my child!' said Cain; 'guide me, little child!' And the innocent little child clasped a finger of the hand which had murdered the righteous Abel, and he guided his father. 'The fir branches drip upon thee, my son.' 'Yea, pleasantly, father, for I ran fast and eagerly to bring thee the pitcher and the cake, and my body is not yet cool. How happy the squirrels are that feed on these fir-trees! they leap from bough to bough, and the old squirrels play round their young ones in the nest. I clomb a tree yesterday at noon, O my father, that I might play with them, but they leaped away from the branches, even to the slender twigs they leap, and in a moment I beheld them on another tree. Why, O my father, would they not play with me? I would be good to them as thou art good to me: and I groaned to them even as thou groanest when thou givest me to eat, and when thou coverest me at evening, and as often as I stand at thy knee and thine eyes look at me?' Then Cain stopped, and stifling his groans he sank to the earth, and the child Enos stood in the darkness beside him.

And Cain lifted up his voice and cried bitterly, and said, 'The Mighty One that persecuteth me is on this side and on that; he pursueth my soul like the wind, like the sand-blast he passeth through me; he is around me even as the air! O that I might be utterly no more! I desire to die – yea, the things that never had life, neither move they upon the earth – behold! they seem precious to mine eyes. O that a man might live without the breath of his nostrils. So I might abide in darkness, and blackness, and an empty space! Yea, I would lie down, I would not rise, neither would I stir my limbs till I became as the rock in the den of the lion, on which the young lion resteth his head whilst he sleepeth. For the torrent that roareth far off hath a voice: and the clouds in heaven look terribly on me; the Mighty One who is against me speaketh in the wind of the cedar grove; and in silence am I dried up.' Then Enos spake to his father, 'Arise, my father, arise, we are but a little way from the place where I found the cake and the pitcher.' And Cain said, 'How knowest thou?' and the child answered – 'Behold the bare rocks are a few of thy strides distant from the forest; and while even now thou wert lifting up thy voice, I heard the echo.' Then the child took hold of his father, as if he would raise him: and Cain being faint and feeble rose slowly on his knees and pressed himself against the trunk of a fir, and stood upright and followed the child.

The path was dark till within three strides' length of its termination, when it turned suddenly; the thick black trees formed a low arch, and the moonlight appeared for a moment like a dazzling portal. Enos ran before and stood in the open air; and when Cain, his father, emerged from the darkness, the child was affrighted. For the mighty limbs of Cain were wasted as by fire; his hair was as the matted curls on the bison's forehead, and so glared his fierce and sullen eye beneath: and the black abundant locks on either side, a rank and tangled mass, were stained and scorched, as though the grasp of a burning iron hand had striven to rend them; and his countenance told in a strange and terrible language of agonies that had been, and were, and were still to continue to be.

The scene around was desolate; as far as the eye could reach it was desolate: the bare rocks faced each other, and left a long and wide interval of thin white sand. You might wander on and look round and round, and peep into the crevices of the rocks and discover nothing that acknowledged the influence of the seasons. There was no spring, no summer, no autumn: and the winter's snow, that would have been lovely, fell not on these hot rocks and scorching sands. Never morning lark had poised himself over this desert; but the huge serpent often hissed there beneath the talons of the vulture, and the vulture screamed, his wings imprisoned within the coils of the serpent. The pointed and shattered summits of the ridges of the rocks made a rude mimicry of human concerns, and seemed to prophesy mutely of things that then were not; steeples, and battlements, and ships with naked masts. As far from the wood as a boy might sling a pebble of the brook, there was one rock by itself at a small distance from the main ridge. It had been precipitated there perhaps by the groan which the Earth uttered when our first father fell. Before you approached, it appeared to lie flat on the ground, but its base slanted from its point, and between its point and the sands a tall man might stand upright. It was here that Enos had found the pitcher and cake, and to this place he led his father. But ere they had reached the rock they beheld a human shape: his back was towards them, and they were advancing unperceived, when they heard him smite his breast and cry aloud, 'Woe is me! woe is me! I must never die again, and yet I am perishing with thirst and hunger.'

Pallid, as the reflection of the sheeted lightning on the heavy-sailing night-cloud, became the face of Cain; but the child Enos took hold of the shaggy skin, his father's robe, and raised his eyes to his father, and listening whispered, 'Ere yet I could speak, I am sure, O my father, that I heard that voice. Have not I often said that I remembered a sweet voice? O my father! this is it': and Cain trembled exceedingly. The voice was sweet indeed, but it was thin and querulous, like that of a feeble slave in misery, who despairs altogether, yet can not refrain himself from weeping and lamentation. And, behold! Enos glided forward, and creeping softly round the base of the rock, stood before the stranger, and looked up into his face. And the Shape shrieked, and turned round, and Cain beheld him, that his limbs and his face were those of his brother Abel whom he had killed! And Cain stood like one who struggles in his sleep because of the exceeding terribleness of a dream.

Thus as he stood in silence and darkness of soul, the Shape fell at his feet, and embraced his knees, and cried out with a bitter outcry, 'Thou eldest born of Adam, whom Eve, my mother, brought forth, cease to torment me! I was feeding my flocks in green pastures by the side of quiet rivers, and thou killedst me; and now I am in misery.' Then Cain closed his eyes, and hid them with his hands; and again he opened his eyes, and looked around him, and said to Enos, 'What beholdest thou? Didst thou hear a voice, my son?' 'Yes, my father, I beheld a man in unclean garments, and he uttered a sweet voice, full of lamentation.' Then

Cain raised up the Shape that was like Abel, and said: – 'The Creator of our father, who had respect unto thee, and unto thy offering, wherefore hath he forsaken thee?' Then the Shape shrieked a second time, and rent his garment, and his naked skin was like the white sands beneath their feet; and he shrieked yet a third time, and threw himself on his face upon the sand that was black with the shadow of the rock, and Cain and Enos sate beside him; the child by his right hand, and Cain by his left. They were all three under the rock, and within the shadow. The Shape that was like Abel raised himself up, and spake to the child: 'I know where the cold waters are, but I may not drink, wherefore didst thou then take away my pitcher?' But Cain said, 'Didst thou not find favour in the sight of the Lord thy God?' The Shape answered, 'The Lord is God of the living only, the dead have another God.' Then the child Enos lifted up his eyes and prayed; but Cain rejoiced secretly in his heart. 'Wretched shall they be all the days of their mortal life,' exclaimed the Shape, 'who sacrifice worthy and acceptable sacrifices to the God of the dead; but after death their toil ceaseth. Woe is me, for I was well beloved by the God of the living, and cruel wert thou, O my brother, who didst snatch me away from his power and his dominion.' Having uttered these words, he rose suddenly, and fled over the sands: and Cain said in his heart, 'The curse of the Lord is on me; but who is the God of the dead?' and he ran after the Shape, and the Shape fled shrieking over the sands, and the sands rose like white mists behind the steps of Cain, but the feet of him that was like Abel disturbed not the sands. He greatly outrun Cain, and turning short, he wheeled round, and came again to the rock where they had been sitting, and where Enos still stood; and the child caught hold of his garment as he passed by, and he fell upon the ground. And Cain stopped, and beholding him not, said, 'he has passed into the dark woods,' and he walked slowly back to the rocks; and when he reached it the child told him that he had caught hold of his garment as he passed by, and that the man had fallen upon the ground: and Cain once more sate beside him, and said, 'Abel, my brother, I would lament for thee, but that the spirit within me is withered, and burnt up with extreme agony. Now, I pray thee, by thy flocks, and by thy pastures, and by the quiet rivers which thou lovedst, that thou tell me all that thou knowest. Who is the God of the dead? where doth he make his dwelling? what sacrifices are acceptable unto him? for I have offered, but have not been received; I have prayed, and have not been heard; and how can I be afflicted more than I already am?' The Shape arose and answered, 'O that thou hadst had pity on me as I will have pity on thee. Follow me, Son of Adam! and bring thy child with thee!'

And they three passed over the white sands between the rocks, silent as the shadows.


[The following notes for a continuation or alternative version of 'The Wanderings of Cain' were found among Coleridge's papers.]

He falls down in a trance – when he awakes he sees a luminous body coming before him. It stands before him an orb of fire. It goes on, he moves not. It returns to him again, again retires as if wishing him to follow it. It then goes on and he follows: they are led to near the bottom of the wild woods, brooks, forests etc. etc. The Fire gradually shapes itself, retaining its luminous appearance, into the lineaments of a man. A dialogue between the fiery shape and Cain, in which the being presses upon him the enormity of his guilt and that he must make some expiation to the true deity, who is a severe God, and persuades him to burn out his eyes. Cain opposes this idea, and says that God himself who had inflicted this punishment upon him, had done it because he neglected to make a proper use of his senses, etc. The evil spirit answers him that God is indeed a God of mercy, and that an example must be given to mankind, that this end will be answered by his terrible appearance, at the same time he will be gratified with the most delicious sights and feelings. Cain, over-persuaded, consents to do it, but wishes to go to the top of the rocks to take a farewell of the earth. His farewell speech concluding with an abrupt address to the promised redeemer, and he abandons the idea on which the being had accompanied him, and turning round to declare this to the being he sees him dancing from rock to rock in his former shape down those interminable precipices.

Child affeared by his father's ravings, goes out to pluck the fruits in the moonlight wildness. Cain's soliloquy. Child returns with a pitcher of water and a cake. Cain wonders what kind of beings dwell in that place – whether any created since man or whether this world had any beings rescued from the Chaos, wandering like shipwrecked beings from another world etc.

Midnight on the Euphrates. Cedars, palms, pines. Cain discovered sitting on the upper part of the ragged rock, where is cavern overlooking the Euphrates, the moon rising on the horizon. His soliloquy. The Beasts are out on the ramp – he hears the screams of a woman and children surrounded by tigers. Cain makes a soliloquy debating whether he shall save the woman. Cain advances, wishing death, and the tigers rush off. It proves to be Cain's wife with her two children, determined to follow her husband. She prevails upon him at last to tell his story. Cain's wife tells him that her son Enoch was placed suddenly by her side. Cain addresses all the elements to cease for a while to persecute him, while he tells his story. He begins with telling her that he had first after his leaving her found out a dwelling in the desart under a juniper tree etc., etc., how he meets in the desart a young man whom upon a nearer approach he perceives to be Abel, on whose countenance appears marks of the greatest misery . . . of another being who had power after his life, greater than Jehovah. He is going to offer sacrifices to this being, and persuades Cain to follow him – he comes to an immense gulph filled with water, whither they descend followed by alligators etc. They go till they come to an immense meadow so surrounded as to be inaccessible, and from its depth so vast that you could not see it from above. Abel offers sacrifice from the blood of his arm. A gleam of light illumines the meadow – the countenance of Abel becomes more beautiful, and his arms glistering – he then persuades Cain to offer sacrifice, for himself and his son Enoch by cutting his child's arm and letting the blood fall from it. Cain is about to do it when Abel himself in his angelic appearance, attended by Michael, is seen in the heavens, whence they sail slowly down. Abel addresses Cain with terror, warning him not to offer up his innocent child. The evil spirit throws off the countenance of Abel, assumes its own shape, flies off pursuing a flying battle with Michael. Abel carries off the child.

# Kubla Khan
## Or, a Vision in a Dream. A Fragment

The following fragment is here published at the request of a poet of great
and deserved celebrity [Lord Byron], and, as far as the Author's own
opinions are concerned, rather as a psychological curiosity, than on the
ground of any supposed *poetic* merits.

In the summer of the year 1797, the Author, then in ill health, had
retired to a lonely farm-house between Porlock and Linton, on the Exmoor
confines of Somerset and Devonshire. In consequence of a slight indisposi-
tion, an anodyne had been prescribed, from the effects of which he fell
asleep in his chair at the moment that he was reading the following
sentence, or words of the same substance, in 'Purchas's Pilgrimage': 'Here
the Khan Kubla commanded a palace to be built, and a stately garden
there-unto. And thus ten miles of fertile ground were inclosed with a wall.'
The Author continued for about three hours in a profound sleep, at least of
the external senses, during which time he has the most vivid confidence,
that he could not have composed less than from two to three hundred
lines; if that indeed can be called composition in which all the images rose
up before him as *things*, with a parallel production of the correspondent
expressions, without any sensation or consciousness of effort. On awak-
ing he appeared to himself to have a distinct recollection of the whole, and
taking his pen, ink, and paper, instantly and eagerly wrote down the lines
that are here preserved. At this moment he was unfortunately called out
by a person on business from Porlock, and detained by him above an hour,
and on his return to his room, found, to his no small surprise and
mortification, that though he still retained some vague and dim recol-
lection of the general purport of the vision, yet, with the exception of some
eight or ten scattered lines and images, all the rest had passed away like
the images on the surface of a stream into which a stone has been cast, but,
alas! without the after restoration of the latter!

> Then all the charm
> Is broken – all that phantom-world so fair
> Vanishes, and a thousand circlets spread,
> And each mis-shape['s] the other. Stay awhile,
> Poor youth! who scarcely dar'st lift up thine eyes –
> The stream will soon renew its smoothness, soon
> The visions will return! And lo, he stays,
> And soon the fragments dim of lovely forms

Come trembling back, unite, and now once more
The pool becomes a mirror.

From *The Picture; or, the Lover's Resolution*, ll. 91–100

Yet from the still surviving recollections in his mind, the Author has frequently purposed to finish for himself what had been originally; as it were, given to him. Σαμερον αδιον ασω: but the to-morrow is yet to come.

[s.t.c.]

In Xanadu did Kubla Khan
A stately pleasure-dome decree:
Where Alph, the sacred river, ran
Through caverns measureless to man
  Down to a sunless sea.
So twice five miles of fertile ground
With walls and towers were girdled round:
And there were gardens bright with sinuous rills,
Where blossomed many an incense-bearing tree;
And here were forests ancient as the hills,
Enfolding sunny spots of greenery.

But oh! that deep romantic chasm which slanted
Down the green hill athwart a cedarn cover!
A savage place! as holy and enchanted
As e'er beneath a waning moon was haunted
By woman wailing for her demon-lover!
  And from this chasm, with ceaseless turmoil seething,
As if this earth in fast thick pants were breathing,
A mighty fountain momently was forced:
Amid whose swift half-intermitted burst
Huge fragments vaulted like rebounding hail,
Or chaffy grain beneath the thresher's flail:
And 'mid these dancing rocks at once and ever
It flung up momently the sacred river.
Five miles meandering with a mazy motion
Through wood and dale the sacred river ran,
Then reached the caverns measureless to man,
And sank in tumult to a lifeless ocean:

118

And 'mid this tumult Kubla heard from far
Ancestral voices prophesying war!
    The shadow of the dome of pleasure
    Floated midway on the waves;
    Where was heard the mingled measure
    From the fountain and the caves.
It was a miracle of rare device,
A sunny pleasure-dome with caves of ice!

    A damsel with a dulcimer
    In a vision once I saw:
    It was an Abyssinian maid,
    And on her dulcimer she played,
    Singing of Mount Abora.
    Could I revive within me
    Her symphony and song,
    To such a deep delight 'twould win me,
That with music loud and long,
I would build that dome in air,
That sunny dome! those caves of ice!
And all who heard should see them there,
And all should cry, Beware! Beware!
His flashing eyes, his floating hair!
Weave a circle round him thrice,
And close your eyes with holy dread,
For he on honey-dew hath fed,
And drunk the milk of Paradise.

# The Ballad of the Dark Ladie
## A Fragment

Beneath yon birch with silver bark,
And boughs so pendulous and fair,
The brook falls scatter'd down the rock:
    And all is mossy there!

And there upon the moss she sits,
The Dark Ladie in silent pain;
The heavy tear is in her eye,
    And drops and swells again.

Three times she sends her little page
Up the castled mountain's breast,
If he might find the Knight that wears
    The Griffin for his crest.

The sun was sloping down the sky,
And she had linger'd there all day,
Counting moments, dreaming fears –
    Oh wherefore can he stay?

She hears a rustling o'er the brook,
She sees far off a swinging bough!
''Tis He! 'Tis my betrothèd Knight!
    Lord Falkland, it is Thou!'

She springs, she clasps him round the neck,
She sobs a thousand hopes and fears,
Her kisses glowing on his cheeks
    She quenches with her tears.

\* \* \*

'My friends with rude ungentle words
They scoff and bid me fly to thee!
O give me shelter in thy breast!
    O shield and shelter me!

'My Henry, I have given thee much,
I gave what I can ne'er recall,
I gave my heart, I gave my peace,
     O Heaven! I gave thee all.'

The Knight made answer to the Maid,
While to his heart he held her hand,
'Nine castles hath my noble sire,
     None statelier in the land.

'The fairest one shall be my love's,
The fairest castle of the nine!
Wait only till the stars peep out,
     The fairest shall be thine:

'Wait only till the hand of eve
Hath wholly closed yon western bars,
And through the dark we two will steal
     Beneath the twinkling stars!' –

'The dark? the dark? No! not the dark?
The twinkling stars? How, Henry? How?
O God! 'twas in the eye of noon
     He pledged his sacred vow!

And in the eye of noon my love
Shall lead me from my mother's door,
Sweet boys and girls all clothed in white
     Strewing flowers before:

But first the nodding minstrels go
With music meet for lordly bowers,
The children next in snow-white vests.
   Strewing buds and flowers!

And then my love and I shall pace,
My jet black hair in pearly braids,
Between our comely bachelors
     And blushing bridal maids.

# The Nightingale
## A Conversation Poem. April 1798

No cloud, no relique of the sunken day
Distinguishes the West, no long thin slip
Of sullen light, no obscure trembling hues.
Come, we will rest on this old mossy bridge!
You see the glimmer of the stream beneath,
But hear no murmuring: it flows silently,
O'er its soft bed of verdure. All is still,
A balmy night! and though the stars be dim,
Yet let us think upon the vernal showers
That gladden the green earth, and we shall find
A pleasure in the dimness of the stars.
And hark! the Nightingale begins its song,
'Most musical, most melancholy' bird!
A melancholy bird? Oh! idle thought!
In nature there is nothing melancholy.
But some night-wandering man, whose heart was pierced
With the remembrance of a grievous wrong,
Or slow distemper, or neglected love,
(And so, poor wretch! filled all things with himself,
And made all gentle sounds tell back the tale
Of his own sorrow) he, and such as he,
First named these notes a melancholy strain.
And many a poet echoes the conceit;
Poet who hath been building up the rhyme
When he had better far have stretched his limbs
Beside a brook in mossy forest-dell,
By sun or moon-light, to the influxes
Of shapes and sounds and shifting elements
Surrendering his whole spirit, of his song
And of his fame forgetful! so his fame
Should share in Nature's immortality,
A venerable thing! and so his song

Should make all Nature lovelier, and itself
Be loved like Nature! But 'twill not be so;
And youths and maidens most poetical,
Who lose the deepening twilights of the spring
In ball-rooms and hot theatres, they still
Full of meek sympathy must heave their sighs
O'er Philomela's pity-pleading strains.

My Friend, and thou, our Sister! we have learnt
A different lore: we may not thus profane
Nature's sweet voices, always full of love
And joyance! 'Tis the merry Nightingale
That crowds, and hurries, and precipitates
With fast thick warble his delicious notes,
As he were fearful that an April night
Would be too short for him to utter forth
His love-chant, and disburthen his full soul
Of all its music!

            And I know a grove
Of large extent, hard by a castle huge,
Which the great lord inhabits not; and so
This grove is wild with tangling underwood,
And the trim walks are broken up, and grass,
Thin grass and king-cups grow within the paths.
But never elsewhere in one place I knew
So many nightingales; and far and near,
In wood and thicket, over the wide grove,
They answer and provoke each other's song,
With skirmish and capricious passagings,
And murmurs musical and swift jug jug,
And one low piping sound more sweet than all –
Stirring the air with such a harmony,
That should you close your eyes, you might almost
Forget it was not day! On moonlight bushes,
Whose dewy leaflets are but half-disclosed,
You may perchance behold them on the twigs,

Their bright, bright eyes, their eyes both bright and full,
Glistening, while many a glow-worm in the shade
Lights up her love-torch.

                              A most gentle Maid,
Who dwelleth in her hospitable home
Hard by the castle, and at latest eve
(Even like a Lady vowed and dedicate
To something more than Nature in the grove)
Glides through the pathways; she knows all their notes,
That gentle Maid! and oft, a moment's space,
What time the moon was lost behind a cloud,
Hath heard a pause of silence; till the moon
Emerging, hath awakened earth and sky
With one sensation, and those wakeful birds
Have all burst forth in choral minstrelsy,
As if some sudden gale had swept at once
A hundred airy harps! And she hath watched
Many a nightingale perch giddily
On blossomy twig still swinging from the breeze,
And to that motion tune his wanton song
Like tipsy Joy that reels with tossing head.

Farewell, O Warbler! till to-morrow eve,
And you, my friends! farewell, a short farewell!
We have been loitering long and pleasantly,
And now for our dear homes. – That strain again!
Full fain it would delay me! My dear babe,
Who, capable of no articulate sound,
Mars all things with his imitative lisp,
How he would place his hand beside his ear,
His little hand, the small forefinger up,
And bid us listen! And I deem it wise
To make him Nature's play-mate. He knows well
The evening-star; and once, when he awoke
In most distressful mood (some inward pain
Had made up that strange thing, an infant's dream –)

I hurried with him to our orchard-plot,
And he beheld the moon, and, hushed at once,
Suspends his sobs, and laughs most silently,
While his fair eyes, that swam with undropped tears,
Did glitter in the yellow moon-beam! Well! –
It is a father's tale: But if that Heaven
Should give me life, his childhood shall grow up
Familiar with these songs, that with the night
He may associate joy. – Once more, farewell,
Sweet Nightingale! once more, my friends! farewell.

# Fire, Famine, and Slaughter
## A War Eclogue

*The Scene a desolated Tract in La Vendée.* FAMINE *is discovered lying on the ground; to her enter* FIRE *and* SLAUGHTER.

FAM.  Sisters! sisters! who sent you here?
SLAU.  (to Fire). I will whisper it in her ear.
FIRE.  No! no! no!
Spirits hear what spirits tell:
'Twill make a holiday in Hell.
No! no! no!
Myself, I named him once below,
And all the souls, that damnèd be,
Leaped up at once in anarchy,
Clapped their hands and danced for glee.
They no longer heeded me;
But laughed to hear Hell's burning rafters
Unwillingly re-echo laughters!
No! no! no!
Spirits hear what spirits tell:
'Twill make a holiday in Hell!
FAM.  Whisper it, sister! so and so!
In a dark hint, soft and slow.
SLAU.  Letters four do form his name –
And who sent you?
BOTH.                          The same! the same!
SLAU.  He came by stealth, and unlocked my den,
And I have drunk the blood since then
Of thrice three hundred thousand men.
BOTH.  Who bade you do't?
SLAU.                          The same! the same!
Letters four do form his name.
He let me loose, and cried Halloo!
To him alone the praise is due.

FAM. Thanks, sister, thanks! the men have bled,
  Their wives and their children faint for bread.
  I stood in a swampy field of battle;
  With bones and skulls I made a rattle,
  To frighten the wolf and carrion-crow
  And the homeless dog – but they would not go.
  So off I flew: for how could I bear
  To see them gorge their dainty fare?
  I heard a groan and a peevish squall,
  And through the chink of a cottage-wall –
  Can you guess what I saw there?

BOTH. Whisper it, sister! in our ear.

FAM. A baby beat its dying mother:
  I had starved the one and was starving the other!

BOTH. Who bade you do't?

FAM.       The same! the same!
  Letters four do form his name.
  He let me loose, and cried, Halloo!
  To him alone the praise is due.

FIRE. Sisters! I from Ireland came!
  Hedge and corn-fields all on flame,
  I triumphed o'er the setting sun!
  And all the while the work was done,
  On as I strode with my huge strides,
  I flung back my head and I held my sides,
  It was so rare a piece of fun
  To see the sweltered cattle run
  With uncouth gallop through the night,
  Scared by the red and noisy light!
  By the light of his own blazing cot
  Was many a naked Rebel shot:
  The house-stream met the flame and hissed,
  While crash! fell in the roof, I wist,
  On some of those old bed-rid nurses,
  That deal in discontent and curses.

BOTH. Who bade you do't?

FIRE.                    The same! the same!
        Letters four do form his name.
        He let me loose, and cried Halloo!
        To him alone the praise is due.
ALL.    He let us loose, and cried Halloo!
        How shall we yield him honour due?
FAM.    Wisdom comes with lack of food.
        I'll gnaw, I'll gnaw the multitude,
        Till the cup of rage o'erbrim:
        They shall seize him and his brood –
SLAU.   They shall tear him limb from limb!
FIRE.   O thankless beldames and untrue!
        And is this all that you can do
        For him, who did so much for you?
        Ninety months he, by my troth!
        Hath richly catered for you both;
        And in an hour would you repay
        An eight years' work? – Away! away!
        I alone am faithful! I
        Cling to him everlastingly.

# The Rime of the Ancient Mariner
## In Seven Parts

ARGUMENT

How a Ship having passed the Line was driven by storms to the cold
Country towards the South Pole; and how from thence she made her
course to the tropical Latitude of the Great Pacific Ocean; and of the
strange things that befell; and in what manner the Ancyent Marinere came
back to his own Country.

## PART I

An ancient Mariner
meeteth three
gallants bidden to a
wedding-feast, and
detaineth one.

It is an ancient Mariner,
And he stoppeth one of three.
'By thy long grey beard and glittering eye,
Now wherefore stopp'st thou me?

The Bridegroom's doors are opened wide,
And I am next of kin;
The guests are met, the feast is set:
May'st hear the merry din.'

He holds him with his skinny hand,
'There was a ship,' quoth he.
'Hold off! unhand me, grey-beard loon!'
Eftsoons his hand dropt he.

The wedding guest
is spellbound by
the eye of the old
seafaring man, and
constrained to hear
his tale.

He holds him with his glittering eye –
The Wedding-Guest stood still,
And listens like a three years' child:
The Mariner hath his will.

The Wedding-Guest sat on a stone:
He cannot choose but hear;
And thus spake on that ancient man,
The bright-eyed Mariner.

'The ship was cheered, the harbour cleared,
Merrily did we drop
Below the kirk, below the hill,
Below the lighthouse top.

The Mariner tells
how the ship sailed
southward with a
good wind and fair
weather, till it
reached the line.

The Sun came up upon the left,
Out of the sea came he!
And he shone bright, and on the right
Went down into the sea.

Higher and higher every day,
Till over the mast at noon –'
The Wedding-Guest here beat his breast,
For he heard the loud bassoon.

The wedding guest
heareth the bridal
music; but the
Mariner continueth
his tale.

The bride hath paced into the hall,
Red as a rose is she;
Nodding their heads before her goes
The merry minstrelsy.

The Wedding-Guest he beat his breast,
Yet he cannot choose but hear;
And thus spake on that ancient man,
The bright-eyed Mariner.

The ship drawn by
a storm toward the
south pole.

And now the STORM-BLAST came, and he
Was tyrannous and strong:
He struck with his o'ertaking wings,
And chased us south along.

With sloping masts and dipping prow,
As who pursued with yell and blow
Still treads the shadow of his foe,
And forward bends his head,
The ship drove fast, loud roared the blast,
And southward aye we fled.

And now there came both mist and snow,
And it grew wondrous cold:

And ice, mast-high, came floating by,
As green as emerald.

The land of ice, and of fearful sounds where no living thing was to be seen.

And through the drifts the snowy clifts
Did send a dismal sheen:
Nor shapes of men nor beasts we ken –
The ice was all between.

The ice was here, the ice was there,
The ice was all around:
It cracked and growled, and roared and howled,
Like noises in a swound!

Till a great sea-bird, called the Albatross, came through the snow-fog, and was received with great joy and hospitality.

At length did cross an Albatross,
Thorough the fog it came;
As if it had been a Christian soul,
We hailed it in God's name.

It ate the food it ne'er had eat,
And round and round it flew.
The ice did split with a thunder-fit;
The helmsman steered us through!

And lo! the Albatross proveth a bird of good omen, and followeth the ship as it returned northward through fog and floating ice.

And a good south wind sprung up behind;
The Albatross did follow,
And every day, for food or play,
Came to the mariner's hollo!

In mist or cloud, on mast or shroud,
It perched for vespers nine;
Whiles all the night, through fog-smoke white,
Glimmered the white Moon-shine.

The ancient Mariner inhospitably killeth the pious bird of good omen.

'God save thee, ancient Mariner!
From the fiends, that plague thee thus! –
Why look'st thou so?' – With my cross-bow
I shot the Albatross.

131

## PART II

The Sun now rose upon the right:
Out of the sea came he,
Still hid in mist, and on the left
Went down into the sea.

And the good south wind still blew behind,
But no sweet bird did follow,
Nor any day for food or play
Came to the mariners' hollo!

The shipmates cry out against the ancient Mariner, for killing the bird of good luck.

And I had done a hellish thing,
And it would work 'em woe:
For all averred, I had killed the bird
That made the breeze to blow.
Ah wretch! said they, the bird to slay,
That made the breeze to blow!

But when the fog cleared off, they justify the same, and thus make themselves accomplices in the crime.

Nor dim nor red, like God's own head,
The glorious Sun uprist:
Then all averred, I had killed the bird
That brought the fog and mist.
'Twas right, said they, such birds to slay,
That bring the fog and mist.

The fair breeze continues; the ship enters the Pacific Ocean, and sails northward, even till it reaches the Line.

The fair breeze blew, the white foam flew,
The furrow followed free;
We were the first that ever burst
Into that silent sea.

The ship hath been suddenly becalmed.

Down dropt the breeze, the sails dropt down,
'Twas sad as sad could be;
And we did speak only to break
The silence of the sea!

All in a hot and copper sky,
The bloody Sun, at noon,
Right up above the mast did stand,
No bigger than the Moon.

Day after day, day after day,
We stuck, nor breath nor motion;
As idle as a painted ship
Upon a painted ocean.

And the Albatross begins to be avenged.

Water, water, every where,
And all the boards did shrink;
Water, water, every where,
Nor any drop to drink.

The very deep did rot: O Christ!
That ever this should be!
Yea, slimy things did crawl with legs
Upon the slimy sea.

About, about, in reel and rout
The death-fires danced at night;
The water, like a witch's oils,
Burnt green, and blue and white.

A Spirit had followed them; one of the invisible inhabitants of this planet, neither departed souls nor angels; concerning whom the learned Jew, Josephus, and the Platonic Constantinopolitan, Michael Psellus, may be consulted. They are very numerous, and there is no climate or element without one or more.

And some in dreams assurèd were
Of the Spirit that plagued us so;
Nine fathom deep he had followed us
From the land of mist and snow.

And every tongue, through utter drought,
Was withered at the root;
We could not speak, no more than if
We had been choked with soot.

The shipmates, in their sore distress, would fain throw the whole guilt on the ancient Mariner: in sign whereof they hang the dead sea-bird round his neck.

Ah! well a-day! what evil looks
Had I from old and young!
Instead of the cross, the Albatross
About my neck was hung.

## PART III

There passed a weary time. Each throat
Was parched, and glazed each eye.
A weary time! a weary time!
How glazed each weary eye,
When looking westward, I beheld
A something in the sky.

At first it seemed a little speck,
And then it seemed a mist;
It moved and moved, and took at last
A certain shape, I wist.

A speck, a mist, a shape, I wist!
And still it neared and neared:
As if it dodged a water-sprite,
It plunged and tacked and veered.

With throats unslaked, with black lips baked,
We could nor laugh nor wail;
Through utter drought all dumb we stood!
I bit my arm, I sucked the blood,
And cried, A sail! a sail!

With throats unslaked, with black lips baked,
Agape they heard me call:
Gramercy! they for joy did grin,
And all at once their breath drew in,
As they were drinking all.

See! see! (I cried) she tacks no more!
Hither to work us weal;
Without a breeze, without a tide,
She steadies with upright keel!

The western wave was all a-flame.
The day was well nigh done!
Almost upon the western wave

*The ancient Mariner beholdeth a sign in the element afar off.*

*At its nearer approach, it seemeth him to be a ship; and at a dear ransom he freeth his speech from the bonds of thirst.*

*A flash of joy;*

*And horror follows. For can it be a ship that comes onward without wind or tide?*

Rested the broad bright Sun;
When that strange shape drove suddenly
Betwixt us and the Sun.

It seemeth him but the skeleton of a ship.

And straight the Sun was flecked with bars,
(Heaven's Mother send us grace!)
As if through a dungeon-grate he peered
With broad and burning face.

Alas! (thought I, and my heart beat loud)
How fast she nears and nears!
Are those *her* sails that glance in the Sun,
Like restless gossameres?

And its ribs are seen as bars on the face of the setting Sun. The spectre-woman and her death-mate, and no other on board the skeleton-ship.

Are those *her* ribs through which the Sun
Did peer, as through a grate?
And is that Woman all her crew?
Is that a Death? and are there two?
Is Death that woman's mate?

Like vessel, like crew!

Death and Life-in-death have diced for the ship's crew, and she (the latter) winneth the ancient Mariner.

*Her* lips were red, *her* looks were free,
Her locks were yellow as gold:
Her skin was as white as leprosy,
The Night-mare Life-in-Death was she,
Who thicks man's blood with cold.

The naked hulk alongside came,
And the twain were casting dice;
'The game is done! I've won! I've won!'
Quoth she, and whistles thrice.

No twilight within the courts of the sun.

The Sun's rim dips; the stars rush out:
At one stride comes the dark;
With far-heard whisper, o'er the sea,
Off shot the spectre-bark.

At the rising of the Moon.

We listened and looked sideways up!
Fear at my heart, as at a cup,
My life-blood seemed to sip!

The stars were dim, and thick the night,
The steersman's face by his lamp gleamed white;
From the sails the dew did drip –
Till clomb above the eastern bar
The hornèd Moon, with one bright star
Within the nether tip.

One after one, by the star-dogged Moon,
Too quick for groan or sigh,
Each turned his face with a ghastly pang,
And cursed me with his eye.

Four times fifty living men,
(And I heard nor sigh nor groan)
With heavy thump, a lifeless lump,
They dropped down one by one.

The souls did from their bodies fly, –
They fled to bliss or woe!
And every soul, it passed me by,
Like the whizz of my cross-bow!

One after another,

His shipmates drop
down dead.

But Life-in-Death
begins her work on
the ancient
Mariner.

## PART IV

'I fear thee, ancient Mariner!
I fear thy skinny hand!
And thou art long, and lank, and brown,
As is the ribbed sea-sand.

I fear thee and thy glittering eye,
And thy skinny hand, so brown.' –
Fear not, fear not, thou Wedding-Guest!
This body dropt not down.

Alone, alone, all, all alone,
Alone on a wide wide sea!
And never a saint took pity on
My soul in agony.

The wedding guest
feareth that a Spirit
is talking to him.

But the ancient
Mariner assureth
him of his bodily
life, and proceedeth
to relate his horrible
penance.

He despiseth the creatures of the calm,

The many men, so beautiful!
And they all dead did lie:
And a thousand thousand slimy things
Lived on; and so did I.

And envieth that they should live, and so many lie dead.

I looked upon the rotting sea,
And drew my eyes away;
I looked upon the rotting deck,
And there the dead men lay.

I looked to heaven, and tried to pray;
But or ever a prayer had gusht,
A wicked whisper came, and made
My heart as dry as dust.

I closed my lids, and kept them close,
And the balls like pulses beat;
For the sky and the sea, and the sea and the sky
Lay like a load on my weary eye,
And the dead were at my feet.

But the curse liveth for him in the eye of the dead men.

The cold sweat melted from their limbs,
Nor rot nor reek did they:
The look with which they looked on me.
Had never passed away.

An orphan's curse would drag to hell
A spirit from on high;
But oh! more horrible than that
Is the curse in a dead man's eye!
Seven days, seven nights, I saw that curse,
And yet I could not die.

In his loneliness and fixedness he yearneth towards the journeying Moon, and the stars that still sojourn, yet still move onward; and every where the blue sky

The moving Moon went up the sky,
And no where did abide:
Softly she was going up,
And a star or two beside –

137

belongs to them,
and is their
appointed rest, and
their native country
and their own
natural homes,
which they enter
unannounced, as
lords that are certainly expected and yet there is a silent joy at their arrival.

Her beams bemocked the sultry main,
Like April hoar-frost spread;
But where the ship's huge shadow lay,
The charmèd water burnt alway
A still and awful red.

By the light of the
Moon he beholdeth
God's creatures of
the great calm.

Beyond the shadow of the ship,
I watched the water-snakes:
They moved in tracks of shining white,
And when they reared, the elfish light
Fell off in hoary flakes.

Within the shadow of the ship
I watched their rich attire:
Blue, glossy green, and velvet black,
They coiled and swam; and every track
Was a flash of golden fire.

Their beauty and
their happiness.

O happy living things! no tongue
Their beauty might declare:
A spring of love gushed from my heart,

He blesseth them
in his heart.

And I blessed them unaware:
Sure my kind saint took pity on me,
And I blessed them unaware.

The spell begins to
break.

The self-same moment I could pray;
And from my neck so free
The Albatross fell off, and sank
Like lead into the sea.

### PART V

Oh sleep! it is a gentle thing,
Beloved from pole to pole!
To Mary Queen the praise be given!
She sent the gentle sleep from Heaven,
That slid into my soul.

By grace of the holy
Mother, the ancient
Mariner is
refreshed with rain.

The silly buckets on the deck,
That had so long remained,
I dreamt that they were filled with dew;
And when I awoke, it rained.

My lips were wet, my throat was cold,
My garments all were dank;
Sure I had drunken in my dreams,
And still my body drank.

I moved, and could not feel my limbs:
I was so light – almost
I thought that I had died in sleep,
And was a blessed ghost.

He heareth sounds
and seeth strange
sights and
commotions in the
sky and the
element.

And soon I heard a roaring wind;
It did not come anear;
But with its sound it shook the sails,
That were so thin and sere.

The upper air burst into life!
And a hundred fire-flags sheen,
To and fro they were hurried about!
And to and fro, and in and out,
The wan stars danced between.

And the coming wind did roar more loud,
And the sails did sigh like sedge;
And the rain poured down from one black cloud;
The Moon was at its edge.

The thick black cloud was cleft, and still
The Moon was at its side:
Like waters shot from some high crag,
The lightning fell with never a jag,
A river steep and wide.

The loud wind never reached the ship,
Yet now the ship moved on!
Beneath the lightning and the Moon
The dead men gave a groan.

They groaned, they stirred, they all uprose,
Nor spake, nor moved their eyes;
It had been strange, even in a dream,
To have seen those dead men rise.

The helmsman steered, the ship moved on;
Yet never a breeze up-blew;
The mariners all 'gan work the ropes,
Where they were wont to do;
They raised their limbs like lifeless tools –
We were a ghastly crew.

The body of my brother's son
Stood by me, knee to knee:
The body and I pulled at one rope,
But he said nought to me.

'I fear thee, ancient Mariner!'
Be calm, thou Wedding-Guest!
'Twas not those souls that fled in pain,
Which to their corses came again,
But a troop of spirits blest:

For when it dawned – they dropped their arms,
And clustered round the mast;
Sweet sounds rose slowly through their mouths,
And from their bodies passed.

Around, around, flew each sweet sound,
Then darted to the Sun;
Slowly the sounds came back again,
Now mixed, now one by one.

Sometimes a-dropping from the sky
I heard the sky-lark sing;

Sometimes all little birds that are,
How they seemed to fill the sea and air
With their sweet jargoning!

And now 'twas like all instruments,
Now like a lonely flute;
And now it is an angel's song,
That makes the heavens be mute.

It ceased; yet still the sails made on
A pleasant noise till noon,
A noise like of a hidden brook
In the leafy month of June,
That to the sleeping woods all night
Singeth a quiet tune.

Till noon we quietly sailed on,
Yet never a breeze did breathe:
Slowly and smoothly went the ship,
Moved onward from beneath.

The lonesome Spirit from the south-pole carries on the ship as far as the Line, in obedience to the angelic troop, but still requireth vengeance.

Under the keel nine fathom deep,
From the land of mist and snow,
The Spirit slid: and it was he
That made the ship to go.
The sails at noon left off their tune,
And the ship stood still also.

The Sun, right up above the mast,
Had fixed her to the ocean:
But in a minute she 'gan stir,
With a short uneasy motion –
Backwards and forwards half her length
With a short uneasy motion.

Then like a pawing horse let go,
She made a sudden bound:
It flung the blood into my head,
And I fell down in a swound.

141

The Polar Spirit's
fellow-daemons, the
invisible inhabitants
of the element, take
part in his wrong;
and two of them
relate, one to the
other, that penance
long and heavy for
the ancient Mariner
hath been accorded
to the Polar Spirit,
who returneth
southward.

How long in that same fit I lay,
I have not to declare;
But ere my living life returned,
I heard, and in my soul discerned
Two voices in the air.

'Is it he?' quoth one, 'Is this the man?
By him who died on cross,
With his cruel bow he laid full low
The harmless Albatross.

The Spirit who bideth by himself
In the land of mist and snow,
He loved the bird that loved the man
Who shot him with his bow.'

The other was a softer voice,
As soft as honey-dew:
Quoth he, 'The man hath penance done,
And penance more will do.'

## PART VI

FIRST VOICE
'But tell me, tell me! speak again,
Thy soft response renewing –
What makes that ship drive on so fast?
What is the ocean doing?'

SECOND VOICE
'Still as a slave before his lord,
The ocean hath no blast;
His great bright eye most silently
Up to the Moon is cast –

If he may know which way to go;
For she guides him smooth or grim.
See, brother, see! how graciously
She looketh down on him.'

The Mariner hath
been cast into a
trance; for the
angelic power
causeth the vessel
to drive northward
faster than human
life could endure.

'But why drives on that ship so fast,
Without or wave or wind?'

SECOND VOICE
'The air is cut away before,
And closes from behind.

Fly, brother, fly! more high, more high!
Or we shall be belated:
For slow and slow that ship will go,
When the Mariner's trance is abated.'

The supernatural
motion is retarded;
the Mariner awakes,
and his penance
begins anew.

I woke, and we were sailing on
As in a gentle weather:
'Twas night, calm night, the moon was high;
The dead men stood together.

All stood together on the deck,
For a charnel-dungeon fitter:
All fixed on me their stony eyes,
That in the Moon did glitter.

The pang, the curse, with which they died,
Had never passed away:
I could not draw my eyes from theirs,
Nor turn them up to pray.

The curse is finally
expiated.

And now this spell was snapt: once more
I viewed the ocean green,
And looked far forth, yet little saw
Of what had else been seen –

Like one, that on a lonesome road
Doth walk in fear and dread,
And having once turned round walks on,
And turns no more his head;
Because he knows, a frightful fiend
Doth close behind him tread.

But soon there breathed a wind on me,
Nor sound nor motion made:
Its path was not upon the sea,
In ripple or in shade.

It raised my hair, it fanned my cheek
Like a meadow-gale of spring –
It mingled strangely with my fears,
Yet it felt like a welcoming.

Swiftly, swiftly flew the ship,
Yet she sailed softly too:
Sweetly, sweetly blew the breeze –
On me alone it blew.

*And the ancient Mariner beholdeth his native country.*

Oh! dream of joy! is this indeed
The light-house top I see?
Is this the hill? is this the kirk?
Is this mine own countree?

We drifted o'er the harbour-bar,
And I with sobs did pray –
O let me be awake, my God!
Or let me sleep alway.

The harbour-bay was clear as glass,
So smoothly it was strewn!
And on the bay the moonlight lay,
And the shadow of the Moon.

The rock shone bright, the kirk no less,
That stands above the rock:
The moonlight steeped in silentness
The steady weathercock.

*The angelic spirits leave the dead bodies,*

And the bay was white with silent light,
Till rising from the same,
Full many shapes, that shadows were,
In crimson colours came.

And appear in their own forms of light.

A little distance from the prow
Those crimson shadows were:
I turned my eyes upon the deck –
Oh, Christ! what saw I there!

Each corse lay flat, lifeless and flat,
And, by the holy rood!
A man all light, a seraph-man,
On every corse there stood.

This seraph-band, each waved his hand:
It was a heavenly sight!
They stood as signals to the land,
Each one a lovely light;

This seraph-band, each waved his hand,
No voice did they impart –
No voice; but oh! the silence sank
Like music on my heart.

But soon I heard the dash of oars,
I heard the Pilot's cheer;
My head was turned perforce away
And I saw a boat appear.

The Pilot and the Pilot's boy,
I heard them coming fast:
Dear Lord in Heaven! it was a joy
The dead men could not blast.

I saw a third – I heard his voice:
It is the Hermit good!
He singeth loud his godly hymns
That he makes in the wood.
He'll shrieve my soul, he'll wash away
The Albatross's blood.

## PART VII

The Hermit of the wood,

This Hermit good lives in that wood
Which slopes down to the sea.
How loudly his sweet voice he rears!
He loves to talk with marineres
That come from a far countree.

He kneels at morn, and noon, and eve –
He hath a cushion plump:
It is the moss that wholly hides
The rotted old oak-stump.

The skiff-boat neared: I heard them talk,
'Why, this is strange, I trow!
Where are those lights so many and fair,
That signal made but now?'

Approacheth the ship with wonder.

'Strange, by my faith!' the Hermit said –
'And they answered not our cheer!
The planks looked warped! and see those sails,
How thin they are and sere!
I never saw aught like to them,
Unless perchance it were

Brown skeletons of leaves that lag
My forest-brook along;
When the ivy-tod is heavy with snow,
And the owlet whoops to the wolf below,
That eats the she-wolf's young.'

'Dear Lord! it hath a fiendish look –
(The Pilot made reply)
I am a-feared' – 'Push on, push on!'
Said the Hermit cheerily.

The boat came closer to the ship,
But I nor spake nor stirred;
The boat came close beneath the ship,
And straight a sound was heard.

146

The ship suddenly sinketh.

Under the water it rumbled on,
Still louder and more dread:
It reached the ship, it split the bay;
The ship went down like lead.

The ancient Mariner is saved in the Pilot's boat.

Stunned by that loud and dreadful sound,
Which sky and ocean smote,
Like one that hath been seven days drowned
My body lay afloat;
But swift as dreams, myself I found
Within the Pilot's boat.

Upon the whirl, where sank the ship,
The boat spun round and round;
And all was still, save that the hill
Was telling of the sound.

I moved my lips – the Pilot shrieked
And fell down in a fit;
The holy Hermit raised his eyes,
And prayed where he did sit.

I took the oars: the Pilot's boy,
Who now doth crazy go,
Laughed loud and long, and all the while
His eyes went to and fro.
'Ha! ha!' quoth he, 'full plain I see,
The Devil knows how to row.'

And now, all in my own countree,
I stood on the firm land!
The Hermit stepped forth from the boat,
And scarcely he could stand.

The ancient Mariner earnestly entreateth the Hermit to shrieve him; and the penance of life falls on him.

'O shrieve me, shrieve me, holy man!'
The Hermit crossed his brow.
'Say quick,' quoth he, 'I bid thee say –
What manner of man art thou?'

Forthwith this frame of mine was wrenched
With a woful agony,
Which forced me to begin my tale;
And then it left me free.

And ever and anon
throughout his
future life an agony
constraineth him to
travel from land to
land;

Since then, at an uncertain hour,
That agony returns:
And till my ghastly tale is told,
This heart within me burns.

I pass, like night, from land to land;
I have strange power of speech;
That moment that his face I see,
I know the man that must hear me:
To him my tale I teach.

What loud uproar bursts from that door!
The wedding-guests are there:
But in the garden-bower the bride
And bride-maids singing are:
And hark the little vesper bell,
Which biddeth me to prayer!

O Wedding-Guest! this soul hath been
Alone on a wide wide sea:
So lonely 'twas, that God himself
Scarce seemèd there to be.

O sweeter than the marriage-feast,
'Tis sweeter far to me,
To walk together to the kirk
With a goodly company! –

To walk together to the kirk,
And all together pray,
While each to his great Father bends,
Old men, and babes, and loving friends
And youths and maidens gay!

Farewell, farewell! but this I tell
To thee, thou Wedding-Guest!
He prayeth well, who loveth well
Both man and bird and beast.

He prayeth best, who loveth best
All things both great and small;
For the dear God who loveth us,
He made and loveth all.

The Mariner, whose eye is bright,
Whose beard with age is hoar,
Is gone: and now the Wedding-Guest
Turned from the bridegroom's door.

He went like one that hath been stunned,
And is of sense forlorn:
A sadder and a wiser man,
He rose the morrow morn.

# Lewti
## Or the Circassian Love-Chaunt

At midnight by the stream I roved,
To forget the form I loved.
Image of Lewti! from my mind
Depart; for Lewti is not kind.
The Moon was high, the moonlight gleam
   And the shadow of a star
Heaved upon Tamaha's stream;
   But the rock shone brighter far,
The rock half sheltered from my view
By pendent boughs of tressy yew. –
So shines my Lewti's forehead fair,
Gleaming through her sable hair.
Image of Lewti! from my mind
Depart; for Lewti is not kind.

I saw a cloud of palest hue,
   Onward to the moon it passed;
Still brighter and more bright it grew,
With floating colours not a few,
   Till it reached the moon at last:
Then the cloud was wholly bright,
With a rich and amber light!
And so with many a hope I seek,
   And with such joy I find my Lewti;
And even so my pale wan cheek
   Drinks in as deep a flush of beauty!
Nay, treacherous image! leave my mind,
If Lewti never will be kind.

The little cloud – it floats away,
   Away it goes; away so soon!
Alas! it has no power to stay:

Its hues are dim, its hues are grey –
   Away it passes from the moon!
How mournfully it seems to fly,
   Ever fading more and more,
To joyless regions of the sky –
   And now 'tis whiter than before!
As white as my poor cheek will be,
   When, Lewti! on my couch I lie,
A dying man for love of thee.
Nay, treacherous image! leave my mind –
And yet, thou didst not look unkind.

I saw a vapour in the sky,
Thin, and white, and very high;
I ne'er beheld so thin a cloud:
   Perhaps the breezes that can fly
   Now below and now above,
Have snatched aloft the lawny shroud
   Of Lady fair – that died for love.
For maids, as well as youths, have perished
From fruitless love too fondly cherished.
Nay, treacherous image! leave my mind –
For Lewti never will be kind.

Hush! my heedless feet from under
   Slip the crumbling banks for ever:
Like echoes to a distant thunder,
   They plunge into the gentle river.
The river-swans have heard my tread,
And startle from their reedy bed.
O beauteous birds! methinks ye measure
   Your movements to some heavenly tune!
O beauteous birds! 'tis such a pleasure
   To see you move beneath the moon,
I would it were your true delight
To sleep by day and wake all night.

I know the place where Lewti lies,
When silent night has closed her eyes:
   It is a breezy jasmine-bower,
The nightingale sings o'er her head:
   Voice of the Night! had I the power
That leafy labyrinth to thread,
And creep, like thee, with soundless tread,
I then might view her bosom white
Heaving lovely to my sight,
As these two swans together heave
On the gently-swelling wave.

Oh! that she saw me in a dream,
   And dreamt that I had died for care;
All pale and wasted I would seem,
   Yet fair withal, as spirits are!
I'd die indeed, if I might see
Her bosom heave, and heave for me!
Soothe, gentle image! soothe my mind!
To-morrow Lewti may be kind.

# Christabel
## Preface

The first part of the following poem was written in the year 1797, at Stowey, in the county of Somerset. The second part, after my return from Germany, in the year 1800, at Keswick, Cumberland. It is probable that if the poem had been finished at either of the former periods, or if even the first and second part had been published in the year 1800, the impression of its originality would have been much greater than I dare at present expect. But for this I have only my own indolence to blame. The dates are mentioned for the exclusive purpose of precluding charges of plagiarism or servile imitation for myself. For there is amongst us a set of critics, who seem to hold, that every possible thought and image is traditional; who have no notion that there are such things as fountains in the world, small as well as great; and who would therefore charitably derive every rill they behold flowing, from a perforation made in some other man's tank. I am confident, however, that as far as the present poem is concerned, the celebrated poets whose writings I might be suspected of having imitated, either in particular passages, or in the tone and the spirit of the whole, would be among the first to vindicate me from the charge, and who, on any striking coincidence, would permit me to address them in this doggerel version of two monkish Latin hexameters.

> 'Tis mine and it is likewise yours;
> But an if this will not do;
> Let it be mine, good friend! for I
> Am the poorer of the two.

I have only to add that the metre of the Christabel is not, properly speaking, irregular, though it may seem so from its being founded on a new principle: namely, that of counting in each line the accents, not the syllables. Though the latter may vary from seven to twelve, yet in each line the accents will be found to be only four. Nevertheless, the occasional variation in number of syllables is not introduced wantonly, or for the mere ends of convenience, but in correspondence with some transition, in the nature of the imagery or passion.

[S.T.C.]

## PART I

'Tis the middle of night by the castle clock,
And the owls have awakened the crowing cock;
Tu-whit! – Tu-whoo!
And hark, again! the crowing cock,
How drowsily it crew.

Sir Leoline, the Baron rich,
Hath a toothless mastiff bitch;
From her kennel beneath the rock
She maketh answer to the clock,
Four for the quarters, and twelve for the hour;
Ever and aye, by shine and shower,
Sixteen short howls, not over loud;
Some say, she sees my lady's shroud.

Is the night chilly and dark?
The night is chilly, but not dark.
The thin gray cloud is spread on high,
It covers but not hides the sky.
The moon is behind, and at the full;
And yet she looks both small and dull.
The night is chill, the cloud is gray:
'Tis a month before the month of May,
And the Spring comes slowly up this way.

The lovely lady, Christabel,
Whom her father loves so well,
What makes her in the wood so late,
A furlong from the castle gate?
She had dreams all yesternight
Of her own betrothèd knight;
And she in the midnight wood will pray
For the weal of her lover that's far away.

She stole along, she nothing spoke,
The sighs she heaved were soft and low,

And naught was green upon the oak
But moss and rarest mistletoe:
She kneels beneath the huge oak tree,
And in silence prayeth she.

The lady sprang up suddenly,
The lovely lady, Christabel!
It moaned as near, as near can be,
But what it is, she cannot tell. –
On the other side it seems to be,
Of the huge, broad-breasted, old oak tree.

The night is chill; the forest bare;
Is it the wind that moaneth bleak?
There is not wind enough in the air
To move away the ringlet curl
From the lovely lady's cheek –
There is not wind enough to twirl
The one red leaf, the last of its clan,
That dances as often as dance it can,
Hanging so light, and hanging so high,
On the topmost twig that looks up at the sky.

Hush, beating heart of Christabel!
Jesu, Maria, shield her well!
She folded her arms beneath her cloak,
And stole to the other side of the oak.
        What sees she there?

There she sees a damsel bright,
Drest in a silken robe of white,
That shadowy in the moonlight shone:
The neck that made that white robe wan,
Her stately neck, and arms were bare;
Her blue-veined feet unsandal'd were,
And wildly glittered here and there
The gems entangled in her hair.
I guess, 'twas frightful there to see

A lady so richly clad as she –
Beautiful exceedingly!

Mary mother, save me now!
(Said Christabel). And who art thou?

The lady strange made answer meet,
And her voice was faint and sweet; –
Have pity on my sore distress,
I scarce can speak for weariness:
Stretch forth thy hand, and have no fear!
Said Christabel, How camest thou here?
And the lady, whose voice was faint and sweet,
Did thus pursue her answer meet: –

My sire is of a noble line,
And my name is Geraldine:
Five warriors seized me yestermorn,
Me, even me, a maid forlorn:
They choked my cries with force and fright,
And tied me on a palfrey white.
The palfrey was as fleet as wind,
And they rode furiously behind.
They spurred amain, their steeds were white:
And once we crossed the shade of night.
As sure as Heaven shall rescue me,
I have no thought what men they be;
Nor do I know how long it is
(For I have lain entranced I wis)
Since one, the tallest of the five,
Took me from the palfrey's back,
A weary woman, scarce alive.
Some muttered words his comrades spoke:
He placed me underneath this oak;
He swore they would return with haste;
Whither they went I cannot tell –
I thought I heard, some minutes past,

Sounds as of a castle bell.
Stretch forth thy hand (thus ended she),
And help a wretched maid to flee.

Then Christabel stretched forth her hand,
And comforted fair Geraldine:
O well, bright dame! may you command
The service of Sir Leoline;
And gladly our stout chivalry
Will he send forth and friends withal
To guide and guard you safe and free
Home to your noble father's hall.

She rose: and forth with steps they passed
That strove to be, and were not, fast.
Her gracious stars the lady blest,
And thus spake on sweet Christabel:
All our household are at rest,
The hall as silent as the cell;
Sir Leoline is weak in health,
And may not well awakened be,
But we will move as if in stealth,
And I beseech your courtesy,
This night, to share your couch with me.

They crossed the moat, and Christabel
Took the key that fitted well;
A little door she opened straight,
All in the middle of the gate;
The gate that was ironed within and without,
Where an army in battle array had marched out.
The lady sank, belike through pain,
And Christabel with might and main
Lifted her up, a weary weight,
Over the threshold of the gate:
Then the lady rose again,
And moved, as she were not in pain.

So free from danger, free from fear,
They crossed the court: right glad they were.
And Christabel devoutly cried
To the lady by her side,
Praise we the Virgin all divine
Who hath rescued thee from thy distress!
Alas, alas! said Geraldine,
I cannot speak for weariness.
So free from danger, free from fear,
They crossed the court: right glad they were.

Outside her kennel the mastiff old
Lay fast asleep, in moonshine cold.
The mastiff old did not awake,
Yet she an angry moan did make!
And what can ail the mastiff bitch?
Never till now she uttered yell
Beneath the eye of Christabel.
Perhaps it is the owlet's scritch:
For what can ail the mastiff bitch?

They passed the hall, that echoes still,
Pass as lightly as you will!
The brands were flat, the brands were dying,
Amid their own white ashes lying;
But when the lady passed, there came
A tongue of light, a fit of flame;
And Christabel saw the lady's eye,
And nothing else saw she thereby,
Save the boss of the shield of Sir Leoline tall,
Which hung in a murky old niche in the wall.
O softly tread, said Christabel,
My father seldom sleepeth well.

Sweet Christabel her feet doth bare,
And jealous of the listening air
They steal their way from stair to stair,

Now in glimmer, and now in gloom,
And now they pass the Baron's room,
As still as death with stifled breath!
And now have reached her chamber door;
And now doth Geraldine press down
The rushes of the chamber floor.

The moon shines dim in the open air,
And not a moonbeam enters here.
But they without its light can see
The chamber carved so curiously,
Carved with figures strange and sweet,
All made out of the carver's brain,
For a lady's chamber meet:
The lamp with twofold silver chain
Is fastened to an angel's feet.

The silver lamp burns dead and dim;
But Christabel the lamp will trim.
She trimmed the lamp, and made it bright,
And left it swinging to and fro,
While Geraldine, in wretched plight,
Sank down upon the floor below.

O weary lady, Geraldine,
I pray you, drink this cordial wine!
It is a wine of virtuous powers;
My mother made it of wild flowers.

And will your mother pity me,
Who am a maiden most forlorn?
Christabel answered – Woe is me!
She died the hour that I was born.
I have heard the grey-haired friar tell
How on her death-bed she did say,
That she should hear the castle-bell
Strike twelve upon my wedding-day.

O mother dear! that thou wert here!
I would, said Geraldine, she were!

But soon with altered voice, said she –
'Off, wandering mother! Peak and pine!
I have power to bid thee flee.'
Alas! what ails poor Geraldine?
Why stares she with unsettled eye?
Can she the bodiless dead espy?
And why with hollow voice cries she,
'Off, woman, off! this hour is mine –
Though thou her guardian spirit be,
Off, woman, off! 'tis given to me.'

Then Christabel knelt by the lady's side,
And raised to heaven her eyes so blue –
Alas! said she, this ghastly ride –
Dear lady! it hath wildered you!
The lady wiped her moist cold brow,
And faintly said, ''tis over now!'

Again the wild-flower wine she drank:
Her fair large eyes 'gan glitter bright,
And from the floor whereon she sank,
The lofty lady stood upright:
She was most beautiful to see,
Like a lady of a far countree.

And thus the lofty lady spake –
'All they, who live in the upper sky,
Do love you, holy Christabel!
And you love them, and for their sake
And for the good which me befel,
Even I in my degree will try,
Fair maiden, to requite you well.
But now unrobe yourself; for I
Must pray, ere yet in bed I lie.'

Quoth Christabel, so let it be!
And as the lady bade, did she.
Her gentle limbs did she undress,
And lay down in her loveliness.

But through her brain of weal and woe
So many thoughts moved to and fro,
That vain it were her lids to close;
So half-way from the bed she rose,
And on her elbow did recline
To look at the lady Geraldine.

Beneath the lamp the lady bowed,
And slowly rolled her eyes around;
Then drawing in her breath aloud,
Like one that shuddered, she unbound
The cincture from beneath her breast:
Her silken robe, and inner vest,
Dropt to her feet, and full in view,
Behold! her bosom and half her side –
A sight to dream of, not to tell!
O shield her! shield sweet Christabel!

Yet Geraldine nor speaks nor stirs;
Ah! what a stricken look was hers!
Deep from within she seems half-way
To lift some weight with sick assay,
And eyes the maid and seeks delay;
Then suddenly, as one defied,
Collects herself in scorn and pride,
And lay down by the maiden's side!—
And in her arms the maid she took,
        Ah wel-a-day!
And with low voice and doleful look
These words did say:
'In the touch of this bosom there worketh a spell,
Which is lord of thy utterance, Christabel!

Thou knowest to-night, and wilt know to-morrow,
This mark of my shame, this seal of my sorrow;
     But vainly thou warrest,
          For this is alone in
     Thy power to declare,
          That in the dim forest
     Thou heard'st a low moaning,
And found'st a bright lady, surpassingly fair;
And didst bring her home with thee in love and in
     charity,
To shield her and shelter her from the damp air.'


THE CONCLUSION TO PART I

It was a lovely sight to see
The lady Christabel, when she
Was praying at the old oak tree.
     Amid the jagged shadows
     Of mossy leafless boughs,
     Kneeling in the moonlight,
     To make her gentle vows;
Her slender palms together prest,
Heaving sometimes on her breast;
Her face resigned to bliss or bale –
Her face, oh call it fair not pale,
And both blue eyes more bright than clear,
Each about to have a tear.

With open eyes (ah woe is me!)
Asleep, and dreaming fearfully,
Fearfully dreaming, yet I wis,
Dreaming that alone, which is –
O sorrow and shame! Can this be she,
The lady, who knelt at the old oak tree?
And lo! the worker of these harms,
That holds the maiden in her arms,

162

Seems to slumber still and mild,
As a mother with her child.

A star hath set, a star hath risen,
O Geraldine! since arms of thine
Have been the lovely lady's prison.
O Geraldine! one hour was thine –
Thou'st had thy will! By tairn and rill,
The night-birds all that hour were still.
But now they are jubilant anew,
From cliff and tower, tu-whoo! tu-whoo!
Tu-whoo! tu-whoo! from wood and fell!

And see! the lady Christabel
Gathers herself from out her trance;
Her limbs relax, her countenance
Grows sad and soft; the smooth thin lids
Close o'er her eyes; and tears she sheds –
Large tears that leave the lashes bright!
And oft the while she seems to smile
As infants at a sudden light!

Yea, she doth smile, and she doth weep,
Like a youthful hermitess,
Beauteous in a wilderness,
Who, praying always, prays in sleep.
And, if she move unquietly,
Perchance, 'tis but the blood so free
Comes back and tingles in her feet.
No doubt, she hath a vision sweet.
What if her guardian spirit 'twere,
What if she knew her mother near?
But this she knows, in joys and woes,
That saints will aid if men will call:
For the blue sky bends over all!

## PART II

Each matin bell, the Baron saith,
Knells us back to a world of death.
These words Sir Leoline first said,
When he rose and found his lady dead:
These words Sir Leoline will say
Many a morn to his dying day!

And hence the custom and law began,
That still at dawn the sacristan,
Who duly pulls the heavy bell,
Five and forty beads must tell
Between each stroke – a warning knell,
Which not a soul can choose but hear
From Bratha Head to Wyndermere.

Saith Bracy the bard, So let it knell!
And let the drowsy sacristan
Still count as slowly as he can!
There is no lack of such, I ween,
As well fill up the space between.
In Langdale Pike and Witch's Lair,
And Dungeon-ghyll so foully rent,
With ropes of rock and bells of air
Three sinful sextons' ghosts are pent,
Who all give back, one after t'other,
The death-note to their living brother;
And oft too, by the knell offended,
Just as their one! two! three! is ended,
The devil mocks the doleful tale
With a merry peal from Borodale.

The air is still! through mist and cloud
That merry peal comes ringing loud;
And Geraldine shakes off her dread,
And rises lightly from the bed;

Puts on her silken vestments white,
And tricks her hair in lovely plight,
And nothing doubting of her spell
Awakens the lady Christabel.
'Sleep you, sweet lady Christabel?
I trust that you have rested well.'

And Christabel awoke and spied
The same who lay down by her side –
O rather say, the same whom she
Raised up beneath the old oak tree!
Nay, fairer yet! and yet more fair!
For she belike hath drunken deep
Of all the blessedness of sleep!
And while she spake, her looks, her air
Such gentle thankfulness declare,
That (so it seemed) her girded vests
Grew tight beneath her heaving breasts.
'Sure I have sinn'd!' said Christabel,
'Now heaven be praised if all be well!'
And in low faltering tones, yet sweet,
Did she the lofty lady greet
With such perplexity of mind
As dreams too lively leave behind.

So quickly she rose, and quickly arrayed
Her maiden limbs, and having prayed
That He, who on the cross did groan,
Might wash away her sins unknown,
She forthwith led fair Geraldine
To meet her sire, Sir Leoline.

The lovely maid and the lady tall
Are pacing both into the hall,
And pacing on through page and groom,
Enter the Baron's presence-room.

The Baron rose, and while he prest
His gentle daughter to his breast,
With cheerful wonder in his eyes
The lady Geraldine espies,
And gave such welcome to the same,
As might beseem so bright a dame!

But when he heard the lady's tale,
And when she told her father's name,
Why waxed Sir Leoline so pale,
Murmuring o'er the name again,
Lord Roland de Vaux of Tryermaine?

Alas! they had been friends in youth;
But whispering tongues can poison truth;
And constancy lives in realms above;
And life is thorny; and youth is vain;
And to be wroth with one we love
Doth work like madness in the brain.
And thus it chanced, as I divine,
With Roland and Sir Leoline.
Each spake words of high disdain
And insult to his heart's best brother:
They parted – ne'er to meet again!
But never either found another
To free the hollow heart from paining –
They stood aloof, the scars remaining,
Like cliffs which had been rent asunder;
A dreary sea now flows between; –
But neither heat, nor frost, nor thunder,
Shall wholly do away, I ween,
The marks of that which once hath been.

Sir Leoline, a moment's space,
Stood gazing on the damsel's face:
And the youthful Lord of Tryermaine
Came back upon his heart again.

O then the Baron forgot his age,
His noble heart swelled high with rage;
He swore by the wounds in Jesu's side
He would proclaim it far and wide,
With trump and solemn heraldry,
That they who thus had wronged the dame,
Were base as spotted infamy!
'And if they dare deny the same,
My herald shall appoint a week,
And let the recreant traitors seek
My tourney court – that there and then
I may dislodge their reptile souls
From the bodies and forms of men!'
He spake: his eye in lightning rolls!
For the lady was ruthlessly seized; and he kenned
In the beautiful lady the child of his friend!

And now the tears were on his face,
And fondly in his arms he took
Fair Geraldine, who met the embrace,
Prolonging it with joyous look.
Which when she viewed, a vision fell
Upon the soul of Christabel,
The vision of fear, the touch and pain!
She shrunk and shuddered, and saw again –
(Ah, woe is me! Was it for thee,
Thou gentle maid! such sights to see?)

Again she saw that bosom old,
Again she felt that bosom cold,
And drew in her breath with a hissing sound:
Whereat the Knight turned wildly round,
And nothing saw, but his own sweet maid
With eyes upraised, as one that prayed.

The touch, the sight, had passed away,
And in its stead that vision blest,

Which comforted her after-rest
While in the lady's arms she lay,
Had put a rapture in her breast,
And on her lips and o'er her eyes
Spread smiles like light!
                              With new surprise,
'What ails then my beloved child?'
The Baron said – His daughter mild
Made answer, 'All will yet be well!'
I ween, she had no power to tell
Aught else: so mighty was the spell.

Yet he, who saw this Geraldine,
Had deemed her sure a thing divine:
Such sorrow with such grace she blended,
As if she feared she had offended
Sweet Christabel, that gentle maid!
And with such lowly tones she prayed,
She might be sent without delay
Home to her father's mansion.
                                        'Nay!
Nay, by my soul!' said Leoline.
'Ho! Bracy the bard, the charge be thine!
Go thou, with music sweet and loud,
And take two steeds with trappings proud,
And take the youth whom thou lov'st best
To hear thy harp, and learn thy song,
And clothe you both in solemn vest,
And over the mountains haste along,
Lest wandering folk, that are abroad,
Detain you on the valley road.

'And when he has crossed the Irthing flood,
My merry bard! he hastes, he hastes
Up Knorren Moor, through Halegarth Wood,
And reaches soon that castle good
Which stands and threatens Scotland's wastes.

'Bard Bracy! bard Bracy! your horses are fleet,
Ye must ride up the hall, your music so sweet,
More loud than your horses' echoing feet!
And loud and loud to Lord Roland call,
Thy daughter is safe in Langdale hall!
Thy beautiful daughter is safe and free –
Sir Leoline greets thee thus through me!
He bids thee come without delay
With all thy numerous array
And take thy lovely daughter home:
And he will meet thee on the way .
With all his numerous array
White with their panting palfreys' foam:
And, by mine honour! I will say,
That I repent me of the day
When I spake words of fierce disdain
To Roland de Vaux of Tryermaine! –
– For since that evil hour hath flown,
Many a summer's sun hath shone;
Yet ne'er found I a friend again
Like Roland de Vaux of Tryermaine.'

The lady fell, and clasped his knees,
Her face upraised, her eyes o'erflowing;
And Bracy replied, with faltering voice,
His gracious Hail on all bestowing! –
'Thy words, thou sire of Christabel,
Are sweeter than my harp can tell;
Yet might I gain a boon of thee,
This day my journey should not be,
So strange a dream hath come to me;
That I had vowed with music loud
To clear yon wood from thing unblest,
Warned by a vision in my rest!
For in my sleep I saw that dove,
That gentle bird, whom thou dost love,

And call'st by thy own daughter's name –
Sir Leoline! I saw the same
Fluttering, and uttering fearful moan,
Among the green herbs in the forest alone.
Which when I saw and when I heard,
I wonder'd what might ail the bird;
For nothing near it could I see,
Save the grass and green herbs underneath the old tree.

'And in my dream methought I went
To search out what might there be found;
And what the sweet bird's trouble meant,
That thus lay fluttering on the ground.
I went and peered, and could descry
No cause for her distressful cry;
But yet for her dear lady's sake
I stooped, methought, the dove to take,
When lo! I saw a bright green snake
Coiled around its wings and neck,
Green as the herbs on which it couched,
Close by the dove's its head it crouched;
And with the dove it heaves and stirs,
Swelling its neck as she swelled hers!
I woke; it was the midnight hour,
The clock was echoing in the tower;
But though my slumber was gone by,
This dream it would not pass away –
It seems to live upon my eye!
And thence I vowed this self-same day
With music strong and saintly song
To wander through the forest bare,
Lest aught unholy loiter there.'

Thus Bracy said: the Baron, the while,
Half-listening heard him with a smile;
Then turned to Lady Geraldine,
His eyes made up of wonder and love;

And said in courtly accents fine,
'Sweet maid, Lord Roland's beauteous dove,
With arms more strong than harp or song,
Thy sire and I will crush the snake!'
He kissed her forehead as he spake,
And Geraldine in maiden wise
Casting down her large bright eyes,
With blushing cheek and courtesy fine
She turned her from Sir Leoline;
Softly gathering up her train,
That o'er her right arm fell again;
And folded her arms across her chest,
And couched her head upon her breast,
And looked askance at Christabel –
Jesu, Maria, shield her well!

A snake's small eye blinks dull and shy;
And the lady's eyes they shrunk in her head,
Each shrunk up to a serpent's eye,
And with somewhat of malice, and more of dread,
At Christabel she looked askance! –
One moment – and the sight was fled!
But Christabel in dizzy trance
Stumbling on the unsteady ground
Shuddered aloud, with a hissing sound;
And Geraldine again turned round,
And like a thing, that sought relief,
Full of wonder and full of grief,
She rolled her large bright eyes divine
Wildly on Sir Leoline.

The maid, alas! her thoughts are gone,
She nothing sees – no sight but one!
The maid, devoid of guile and sin,
I know not how, in fearful wise,
So deeply had she drunken in
That look, those shrunken serpent eyes,

That all her features were resigned
To this sole image in her mind:
And passively did imitate
That look of dull and treacherous hate!
And thus she stood, in dizzy trance,
Still picturing that look askance
With forced unconscious sympathy
Full before her father's view –
As far as such a look could be
In eyes so innocent and blue!

And when the trance was o'er, the maid
Paused awhile, and inly prayed:
Then falling at the Baron's feet,
'By my mother's soul do I entreat
That thou this woman send away!'
She said: and more she could not say:
For what she knew she could not tell,
O'er-mastered by the mighty spell.

Why is thy cheek so wan and wild,
Sir Leoline? Thy only child
Lies at thy feet, thy joy, thy pride,
So fair, so innocent, so mild;
The same, for whom thy lady died!
O by the pangs of her dear mother
Think thou no evil of thy child!
For her, and thee, and for no other,
She prayed the moment ere she died:
Prayed that the babe for whom she died,
Might prove her dear lord's joy and pride!
  That prayer her deadly pangs beguiled,
      Sir Leoline!
  And wouldst thou wrong thy only child,
      Her child and thine?

Within the Baron's heart and brain
If thoughts, like these, had any share,
They only swelled his rage and pain,
And did but work confusion there.
His heart was cleft with pain and rage,
His cheeks they quivered, his eyes were wild,
Dishonoured thus in his old age;
Dishonoured by his only child,
And all his hospitality
To the wrong'd daughter of his friend
By more than woman's jealousy
Brought thus to a disgraceful end –
He rolled his eye with stern regard
Upon the gentle minstrel bard,
And said in tones abrupt, austere –
'Why, Bracy! dost thou loiter here?
I bade thee hence!' The bard obeyed;
And turning from his own sweet maid,
The aged knight, Sir Leoline,
Led forth the lady Geraldine!

### THE CONCLUSION TO PART II

A little child, a limber elf,
Singing, dancing to itself,
A fairy thing with red round cheeks,
That always finds, and never seeks,
Makes such a vision to the sight
As fills a father's eyes with light;
And pleasures flow in so thick and fast
Upon his heart, that he at last
Must needs express his love's excess
With words of unmeant bitterness.
Perhaps 'tis pretty to force together
Thoughts so all unlike each other;
To mutter and mock a broken charm,

To dally with wrong that does no harm.
Perhaps 'tis tender too and pretty
At each wild word to feel within
A sweet recoil of love and pity.
And what, if in a world of sin
(O sorrow and shame should this be true!)
Such giddiness of heart and brain
Comes seldom save from rage and pain,
So talks as it's most used to do.

# The Devil's Thoughts

## I

From his brimstone bed at break of day
A walking the Devil is gone,
To visit his snug little farm the earth,
And see how his stock goes on.

## II

Over the hill and over the dale,
And he went over the plain,
And backward and forward he switched his long tail
As a gentleman switches his cane.

## III

And how then was the Devil drest?
Oh! he was in his Sunday's best:
His jacket was red and his breeches were blue,
And there was a hole where the tail came through.

## IV

He saw a Lawyer killing a Viper
On a dunghill hard by his own stable;
And the Devil smiled, for it put him in mind
Of Cain and his brother, Abel.

## V

He saw an Apothecary on a white horse
    Ride by on his vocations,
And the Devil thought of his old Friend
    Death in the Revelations.

## VI

He saw a cottage with a double coach-house,
    A cottage of gentility;
And the Devil did grin, for his darling sin
    Is pride that apes humility.

## VII

He peep'd into a rich bookseller's shop,
    Quoth he! we are both of one college!
For I sate myself, like a cormorant, once
    Hard by the tree of knowledge.

## VIII

Down the river did glide, with wind and tide,
    A pig with vast celerity;
And the Devil look'd wise as he saw how the while,
It cut its own throat. 'There!' quoth he with a smile,
    'Goes "England's commercial prosperity." '

## IX

As he went through Cold-Bath Fields he saw
    A solitary cell;
And the Devil was pleased, for it gave him a hint
    For improving his prisons in Hell.

## X

He saw a Turnkey in a trice
    Fetter a troublesome blade;
'Nimbly,' quoth he, 'do the fingers move
    If a man be but used to his trade.'

## XI

He saw the same Turnkey unfetter a man,
    With but little expedition,
Which put him in mind of the long debate
    On the Slave-trade abolition.

## XII

He saw an old acquaintance
    As he passed by a Methodist meeting; –
She holds a consecrated key,
    And the devil nods her a greeting.

She turned up her nose, and said,
  'Avaunt! my name's Religion,'
And she looked to Mr —
  And leered like a love-sick pigeon.

He saw a certain minister
  (A minister to his mind)
Go up into a certain House,
  With a majority behind.

The Devil quoted Genesis
  Like a very learnèd clerk,
How 'Noah and his creeping things
  Went up into the Ark.'

He took from the poor,
  And he gave to the rich,
And he shook hands with a Scotchman,
  For he was not afraid of the —

General — burning face
  He saw with consternation,
And back to hell his way did he take,
For the Devil thought by a slight mistake
  It was general conflagration.

# The Knight's Tomb

Where is the grave of Sir Arthur O'Kellyn?
Where may the grave of that good man be? –
By the side of a spring, on the breast of Helvellyn,
Under the twigs of a young birch tree!
The oak that in summer was sweet to hear,
And rustled its leaves in the fall of the year,
And whistled and roared in the winter alone,
Is gone, – and the birch in its stead is grown. –
The Knight's bones are dust,
And his good sword rust; –
His soul is with the saints, I trust.

# Dejection: An Ode

> Late, late yestreen I saw the new Moon,
> With the old Moon in her arms;
> And I fear, I fear, my Master dear!
> We shall have a deadly storm.
> *Ballad of Sir Patrick Spence*

## I

Well! If the Bard was weather-wise, who made
  The grand old ballad of Sir Patrick Spence,
  This night, so tranquil now, will not go hence
Unroused by winds, that ply a busier trade
Than those which would yon cloud in lazy flakes,
Or the dull sobbing draft, that moans and rakes
Upon the strings of this Aeolian lute,
    Which better far were mute.
  For lo! the New-moon winter-bright!
  And overspread with phantom light,
  (With swimming phantom light o'erspread
  But rimmed and circled by a silver thread)
I see the old Moon in her lap, foretelling
  The coming on of rain and squally blast.
And oh! that even now the gust were swelling,
  And the slant night-shower driving loud and fast!
Those sounds which oft have raised me, whilst they awed,
    And sent my soul abroad,
Might now perhaps their wonted impulse give,
Might startle this dull pain, and make it move and live!

## II

A grief without a pang, void, dark, and drear,
  A stifled, drowsy, unimpassioned grief,
  Which finds no natural outlet, no relief,
    In word, or sigh, or tear –
O Lady! in this wan and heartless mood,

To other thoughts by yonder throstle woo'd,
   All this long eve, so balmy and serene,
Have I been gazing on the western sky,
   And its peculiar tint of yellow green:
And still I gaze – and with how blank an eye!
And those thin clouds above, in flakes and bars,
That give away their motion to the stars;
Those stars, that glide behind them or between,
Now sparkling, now bedimmed, but always seen:
Yon crescent Moon, as fixed as if it grew
In its own cloudless, starless lake of blue;
I see them all so excellently fair,
I see, not feel, how beautiful they are!

### III

   My genial spirits fail;
   And what can these avail
To lift the smothering weight from off my breast?
   It were a vain endeavour,
   Though I should gaze for ever
On that green light that lingers in the west:
I may not hope from outward forms to win
The passion and the life, whose fountains are within.

### IV

O Lady! we receive but what we give,
And in our life alone does Nature live:
Ours is her wedding-garment, ours her shroud!
   And would we aught behold, of higher worth,
Than that inanimate cold world allowed
To the poor loveless ever-anxious crowd,
   Ah! from the soul itself must issue forth
A light, a glory, a fair luminous cloud
   Enveloping the Earth –
And from the soul itself must there be sent
   A sweet and potent voice, of its own birth,
Of all sweet sounds the life and element!

## V

O pure of heart! thou need'st not ask of me
What this strong music in the soul may be!
What, and wherein it doth exist,
This light, this glory, this fair luminous mist,
This beautiful and beauty-making power.

Joy, virtuous Lady! Joy that ne'er was given,
Save to the pure, and in their purest hour,
Life, and Life's effluence, cloud at once and shower,
Joy, Lady! is the spirit and the power,
Which wedding Nature to us gives in dower
    A new Earth and new Heaven,
Undreamt of by the sensual and the proud –
Joy is the sweet voice, Joy the luminous cloud –
        We in ourselves rejoice!
And thence flows all that charms or ear or sight,
    All melodies the echoes of that voice,
All colours a suffusion from that light.

There was a time when, though my path was rough,
    This joy within me dallied with distress,
And all misfortunes were but as the stuff
    Whence Fancy made me dreams of happiness:
For hope grew round me, like the twining vine,
And fruits, and foliage, not my own, seemed mine.
But now afflictions bow me down to earth:
Nor care I that they rob me of my mirth;
        But oh! each visitation
Suspends what nature gave me at my birth,
    My shaping spirit of Imagination.
For not to think of what I needs must feel,
    But to be still and patient, all I can;
And haply by abstruse research to steal
    From my own nature all the natural man –
    This was my sole resource, my only plan:

Till that which suits a part infects the whole,
And now is almost grown the habit of my soul.

VII

Hence, viper thoughts, that coil around my mind,
  Reality's dark dream!
I turn from you, and listen to the wind,
 Which long has raved unnoticed. What a scream
Of agony by torture lengthened out
That lute sent forth! Thou Wind, that rav'st without,
 Bare crag, or mountain-tairn,* or blasted tree,
Or pine-grove whither woodman never clomb,
Or lonely house, long held the witches' home,
 Methinks were fitter instruments for thee,
Mad Lutanist! who in this month of showers,
Of dark-brown gardens, and of peeping flowers,
Mak'st Devils' yule, with worse than wintry song,
The blossoms, buds, and timorous leaves among.
 Thou Actor, perfect in all tragic sounds!
Thou mighty Poet, e'en to frenzy bold!
  What tell'st thou now about?
  'Tis of the rushing of an host in rout,
 With groans, of trampled men, with smarting wounds –
At once they groan with pain, and shudder with the cold!
But hush! there is a pause of deepest silence!
 And all that noise, as of a rushing crowd,
With groans, and tremulous shudderings – all is over –
 It tells another tale, with sounds less deep and loud!
  A tale of less affright,
  And tempered with delight,
As Otway's self had framed the tender lay, –
  'Tis of a little child

---

* Tairn is a small lake, generally if not always applied to the lakes up in
the mountains and which are the feeders of those in the valleys. This
address to the Storm-wind, will not appear extravagant to those who
have heard it at night and in a mountainous country. [S.T.C.]

Upon a lonesome wild,
Not far from home, but she hath lost her way:
And now moans low in bitter grief and fear,
And now screams loud, and hopes to make her mother hear.

### VIII

'Tis midnight, but small thoughts have I of sleep:
Full seldom may my friend such vigils keep!
Visit her, gentle Sleep! with wings of healing,
   And may this storm be but a mountain-birth,
May all the stars hang bright above her dwelling,
   Silent as though they watched the sleeping Earth!
      With light heart may she rise,
      Gay fancy, cheerful eyes,
   Joy lift her spirit, joy attune her voice;
To her may all things live, from pole to pole,
Their life the eddying of her living soul!
   O simple spirit, guided from above,
Dear Lady! friend devoutest of my choice,
Thus mayest thou ever, evermore rejoice.

# Work Without Hope

All Nature seems at work. Slugs leave their lair –
The bees are stirring – birds are on the wing –
And Winter slumbering in the open air,
Wears on his smiling face a dream of Spring!
And I the while, the sole unbusy thing,
Nor honey make, nor pair, nor build, nor sing.

   Yet well I ken the banks where amaranths blow,
Have traced the fount whence streams of nectar flow.
Bloom, O ye amaranths! bloom for whom ye may,
For me ye bloom not! Glide, rich streams, away!
With lips unbrightened, wreathless brow, I stroll:
And would you learn the spells that drowse my soul?
Work without hope draws nectar in a sieve,
And hope without an object cannot live.

A SUPPLEMENT OF POEMS

# Music

Hence, soul-dissolving Harmony
    That lead'st th' oblivious soul astray –
Though thou sphere-descended be –
    Hence away! –
Thou mightier Goddess, thou demand'st my lay,
    Born when earth was seiz'd with cholic;
Or as more sapient sages say,
    What time the Legion diabolic
        Compell'd their beings to enshrine
        In bodies vile of herded swine,
        Precipitate adown the steep
        With hideous rout were plunging in the deep,
And hog and devil mingling grunt and yell
    Seiz'd on the ear with horrible obtrusion; –
Then if aright old legendaries tell,
    Wert thou begot by Discord on Confusion!

What though no name's sonorous power
Was given thee at thy natal hour! –
Yet oft I feel thy sacred might,
While concords wing their distant flight.
    Such Power inspires thy holy son
        Sable clerk of Tiverton!
And oft where Otter sports his stream,
I hear thy banded offspring scream.
Thou Goddess! thou inspir'st each throat;
'Tis thou who pour'st the scritch-owl note!
Transported hear'st thy children all
Scrape and blow and squeak and squall;
And while old Otter's steeple rings,
Clappest hoarse thy raven wings!

# Honour

*O, curas hominum! O, quantum est in rebus inane!*

The fervid Sun had more than halv'd the day,
When gloomy on his couch Philedon lay;
His feeble frame consumptive as his purse,
His aching head did wine and women curse;
His fortune ruin'd and his wealth decay'd,
Clamorous his duns, his gaming debts unpaid,
The youth indignant seiz'd his tailor's bill,
And on its back thus wrote with moral quill:
'Various as colours in the rainbow shown,
Or similar in emptiness alone,
How false, how vain are Man's pursuits below!
Wealth, Honour, Pleasure – what can ye bestow?
Yet see, how high and low, and young and old
Pursue the all-delusive power of Gold.
Fond man! should all Peru thy empire own,
For thee tho' all Golconda's jewels shone,
What greater bliss could all this wealth supply?
What, but to eat and drink and sleep and die?
Go, tempt the stormy sea, the burning soil –
Go, waste the night in thought, the day in toil,
Dark frowns the rock, and fierce the tempests rave –
Thy ingots go the unconscious deep to pave!
Or thunder at thy door the midnight train,
Or Death shall knock that never knocks in vain.
Next Honour's sons come bustling on amain:
I laugh with pity at the idle train.
Infirm of soul! who think'st to lift thy name
Upon the waxen wings of human fame, –
Who for a sound, articulated breath –
Gazest undaunted in the face of death!
What art thou but a Meteor's glaring light –

Blazing a moment and then sunk in night?
Caprice which rais'd thee high shall hurl thee low,
Or Envy blast the laurels on thy brow.
To such poor joys could ancient Honour lead
When empty fame was toiling Merit's meed;
To Modern Honour other lays belong;
Profuse of joy and Lord of right and wrong,
Honour can game, drink, riot in the stew,
Cut a friend's throat; – what cannot Honour do?
Ah me! – the storm within can Honour still
For Julio's death, whom Honour made me kill?
Or will this lordly Honour tell the way
To pay those debts, which Honour makes me pay?
Or if with pistol and terrific threats
I make some traveller pay my Honour's debts,
A medicine for this wound can Honour give?
Ah, no! my Honour dies to make my Honour live.
But see! young Pleasure, and her train advance,
And joy and laughter wake the inebriate dance;
Around my neck she throws her fair white arms,
I meet her loves, and madden at her charms.
For the gay grape can joys celestial move,
And what so sweet below as Woman's love?
With such high transport every moment flies,
I curse Experience that he makes me wise;
For at his frown the dear deliriums flew,
And the changed scene now wears a gloomy hue.
A hideous hag th' Enchantress Pleasure seems,
And all her joys appear but feverous dreams.
The vain resolve still broken and still made,
Disease and loathing and remorse invade;
The charm is vanish'd and the bubble's broke, –
A slave to pleasure is a slave to smoke!'

   Such lays repentant did the Muse supply;
When as the Sun was hastening down the sky,
In glittering state twice fifty guineas come, –

His Mother's plate antique had rais'd the sum.
Forth leap'd Philedon of new life possest: –
'Twas Brookes's all till two, – 'twas Hackett's all the rest!

## To the Author of 'The Robbers'

Schiller! that hour I would have wish'd to die.
If thro' the shuddering midnight I had sent
From the dark dungeon of the Tower time-rent
That fearful voice, a famish'd Father's cry –
Lest in some after moment aught more mean
Might stamp me mortal! A triumphant shout
Black Horror scream'd, and all her *goblin* rout
Diminish'd shrunk from the more withering scene!
Ah! Bard tremendous in sublimity!
Could I behold thee in thy loftier mood
Wandering at eve with finely-frenzied eye
Beneath some vast old tempest-swinging wood!
Awhile with mute awe gazing I would brood:
Then weep aloud in a wild ecstasy!

# The Eolian Harp
## Composed at Clevedon, Somersetshire

My pensive Sara! thy soft cheek reclined
Thus on mine arm, most soothing sweet it is
To sit beside our Cot, our Cot o'ergrown
With white-flower'd Jasmin, and the broad-leav'd Myrtle,
(Meet emblems they of Innocence and Love!)
And watch the clouds, that late were rich with light,
Slow saddening round, and mark the star of eve
Serenely brilliant (such should Wisdom be)
Shine opposite! How exquisite the scents
Snatch'd from yon bean-field! and the world *so* hush'd!
The stilly murmur of the distant Sea
Tells us of silence.
              And that simplest Lute,
Placed length-ways in the clasping casement, hark!
How by the desultory breeze caress'd,
Like some coy maid half yielding to her lover,
It pours such sweet upbraiding, as must needs
Tempt to repeat the wrong! And now, its strings
Boldlier swept, the long sequacious notes
Over delicious surges sink and rise,
Such a soft floating witchery of sound
As twilight Elfins make, when they at eve
Voyage on gentle gales from Fairy-Land,
Where Melodies round honey-dropping flowers,
Footless and wild, like birds of Paradise,
Nor pause, nor perch, hovering on untam'd wing!
O! the one Life within us and abroad,
Which meets all motion and becomes its soul,
A light in sound, a sound-like power in light,
Rhythm in all thought, and joyance every where –
Methinks, it should have been impossible
Not to love all things in a world so fill'd;

Where the breeze warbles, and the mute still air
Is Music slumbering on her instrument.

And thus, my Love! as on the midway slope
Of yonder hill I stretch my limbs at noon,
Whilst through my half-clos'd eye-lids I behold
The sunbeams dance, like diamonds, on the main,
And tranquil muse upon tranquillity;
Full many a thought uncall'd and undetain'd,
And many idle flitting phantasies,
Traverse my indolent and passive brain,
As wild and various as the random gales
That swell and flutter on this subject Lute!
And what if all of animated nature
Be but organic Harps diversely fram'd,
That tremble into thought, as o'er them sweeps
Plastic and vast, one intellectual breeze,
At once the Soul of each, and God of all?
But thy more serious eye a mild reproof
Darts, O belovèd Woman! nor such thoughts
Dim and unhallow'd dost thou not reject,
And biddest me walk humbly with my God.
Meek Daughter in the family of Christ!
Well hast thou said and holily disprais'd
These shapings of the unregenerate mind;
Bubbles that glitter as they rise and break
On vain Philosophy's aye-babbling spring.
For never guiltless may I speak of him,
The Incomprehensible! save when with awe
I praise him, and with Faith that inly *feels*;
Who with his saving mercies healèd me,
A sinful and most miserable man,
Wilder'd and dark, and gave me to possess
Peace and this Cot, and thee, heart-honour'd Maid!

# Reflections on Having Left a Place of Retirement

*Sermoni propriora* (Horace)

Low was our pretty Cot: our tallest Rose
Peep'd at the chamber-window. We could hear
At silent noon, and eve, and early morn,
The Sea's faint murmur. In the open air
Our Myrtles blossom'd; and across the porch
Thick Jasmins twined: the little landscape round
Was green and woody, and refresh'd the eye.
It was a spot which you might aptly call
The Valley of Seclusion! Once I saw
(Hallowing his Sabbath-day by quietness)
A wealthy son of Commerce saunter by,
Bristowa's citizen: methought, it calm'd
His thirst of idle gold, and made him muse
With wiser feelings: for he paus'd, and look'd
With a pleas'd sadness, and gaz'd all around,
Then eyed our Cottage, and gaz'd round again,
And sigh'd, and said, it was a Blessèd Place.
And we *were* bless'd. Oft with patient ear
Long-listening to the viewless sky-lark's note
(Viewless, or haply for a moment seen
Gleaming on sunny wings) in whisper'd tones
I've said to my Belovèd, 'Such, sweet Girl!
The inobtrusive song of Happiness,
Unearthly minstrelsy! then only heard
When the Soul seeks to hear; when all is hush'd,
And the Heart listens!'

                But the time, when first
From that low Dell, steep up the stony Mount
I climb'd with perilous toil and reach'd the top,
Oh! what a goodly scene! *Here* the bleak mount,

The bare bleak mountain speckled thin with sheep;
Grey clouds, that shadowing spot the sunny fields;
And river, now with bushy rocks o'er-brow'd,
Now winding bright and full, with naked banks;
And seats, and lawns, the Abbey and the wood,
And cots, and hamlets, and faint city-spire;
The Channel *there*, the Islands and white sails,
Dim coasts, and cloud-like hills, and shoreless Ocean –
It seem'd like Omnipresence! God, methought,
Had built him there a Temple: the whole World
Seem'd *imag'd* in its vast circumference:
No *wish* profan'd my overwhelmèd heart.
Blest hour! It was a luxury, – to be!

    Ah! quiet Dell! dear Cot, and Mount sublime!
I was constrain'd to quit you. Was it right,
While my unnumber'd brethren toil'd and bled,
That I should dream away the entrusted hours
On rose-leaf beds, pampering the coward heart
With feelings all too delicate for use?
Sweet is the tear that from some Howard's eye
Drops on the cheek of one he lifts from earth:
And he that works me good with unmov'd face,
Does it but half: he chills me while he aids,
My benefactor, not my brother man!
Yet even this, this cold beneficence
Praise, praise it, O my Soul! oft as thou scann'st
The sluggard Pity's vision-weaving tribe!
Who sigh for Wretchedness, yet shun the Wretched,
Nursing in some delicious solitude
Their slothful loves and dainty sympathies!
I therefore go, and join head, heart, and hand,
Active and firm, to fight the bloodless fight
Of Science, Freedom, and the Truth in Christ.

Yet oft when after honourable toil
Rests the tir'd mind, and waking loves to dream,

My spirit shall revisit thee, dear Cot!
Thy Jasmin and thy window-peeping Rose,
And Myrtles fearless of the mild sea-air.
And I shall sigh fond wishes – sweet Abode!
Ah! – had none greater! And that all had such!
It might be so – but the time is not yet.
Speed it, O Father! Let thy Kingdom come!

## The Foster-Mother's Tale
### A Dramatic Fragment

FOSTER-MOTHER. I never saw the man whom you describe.

MARIA. 'Tis strange! he spake of you familiarly
  As mine and Albert's common Foster-mother.

FOSTER-MOTHER. Now blessings on the man, whoe'er he be,
  That joined your names with mine! O my sweet lady,
  As often as I think of those dear times
  When you two little ones would stand at eve
  On each side of my chair, and make me learn
  All you had learnt in the day; and how to talk
  In gentle phrase, then bid me sing to you –
  'Tis more like heaven to come than what *has* been!

MARIA. O my dear Mother! this strange man has left me
  Troubled with wilder fancies, than the moon
  Breeds in the love-sick maid who gazes at it,
  Till lost in inward vision, with wet eye
  She gazes idly! – But that entrance, Mother!

FOSTER-MOTHER. Can no one hear? It is a perilous tale!

MARIA. No one.

FOSTER-MOTHER. My husband's father told it me,
  Poor old Leoni! – Angels rest his soul!
  He was a woodman, and could fell and saw
  With lusty arm. You know that huge round beam
  Which props the hanging wall of the old Chapel?
  Beneath that tree, while yet it was a tree,
  He found a baby wrapt in mosses, lined
  With thistle-beards, and such small locks of wool
  As hang on brambles. Well, he brought him home,
  And rear'd him at the then Lord Velez' cost.
  And so the babe grew up a pretty boy,
  A pretty boy, but most unteachable –
  And never learnt a prayer, nor told a bead,
  But knew the names of birds, and mock'd their notes,

And whistled, as he were a bird himself:
And all the autumn 'twas his only play
To get the seeds of wild flowers, and to plant them
With earth and water, on the stumps of trees.
A Friar, who gather'd simples in the wood,
A grey-haired man – he lov'd this little boy,
The boy lov'd him – and, when the Friar taught him,
He soon could write with the pen: and from that time,
Lived chiefly at the Convent or the Castle.
So he became a very learnèd youth.
But Oh! poor wretch! – he read, and read, and read,
Till his brain turn'd – and ere his twentieth year,
He had unlawful thoughts of many things:
And though he prayed, he never lov'd to pray
With holy men, nor in a holy place –
But yet his speech, it was so soft and sweet,
The late Lord Velez ne'er was wearied with him.
And once, as by the north side of the Chapel
They stood together, chain'd in deep discourse,
The earth heav'd under them with such a groan,
That the wall totter'd, and had well-nigh fallen
Right on their heads. My Lord was sorely frighten'd;
A fever seiz'd him, and he made confession
Of all the heretical and lawless talk
Which brought this judgment: so the youth was seiz'd
And cast into that hole. My husband's father
Sobb'd like a child – it almost broke his heart:
And once as he was working in the cellar,
He heard a voice distinctly; 'twas the youth's,
Who sung a doleful song about green fields,
How sweet it were on lake or wild savannah,
To hunt for food, and be a naked man,
And wander up and down at liberty.
He always doted on the youth, and now
His love grew desperate; and defying death,
He made that cunning entrance I describ'd:

And the young man escap'd.

MARIA.                     'Tis a sweet tale:
  Such as would lull a listening child to sleep,
  His rosy face besoil'd with unwiped tears. –
  And what became of him?

FOSTER-MOTHER.           He went on shipboard
  With those bold voyagers, who made discovery
  Of golden lands. Leoni's younger brother
  Went likewise, and when he return'd to Spain,
  He told Leoni, that the poor mad youth,
  Soon after they arriv'd in that new world,
  In spite of his dissuasion, seiz'd a boat,
  And all alone, set sail by silent moonlight
  Up a great river, great as any sea,
  And ne'er was heard of more: but 'tis suppos'd.
  He liv'd and died among the savage men.

# Lines Composed in a Concert-Room

Nor cold, nor stern, my soul! yet I detest
   These scented Rooms, where, to a gaudy throng,
Heaves the proud Harlot her distended breast,
   In intricacies of laborious song.

These feel not Music's genuine power, nor deign
   To melt at Nature's passion-warbled plaint;
But when the long-breathed singer's uptrilled strain
   Bursts in a squall – they gape for wonderment.

Hark! the deep buzz of Vanity and Hate!
   Scornful, yet envious, with self-torturing sneer
My lady eyes some maid of humbler state,
   While the pert Captain, or the primmer Priest,
   Prattles accordant scandal in her ear.

O give me, from this heartless scene released,
   To hear our old Musician, blind and grey,
(Whom stretching from my nurse's arms I kissed)
   His Scottish tunes and warlike marches play,
By moonshine, and the balmy summer-night,
   The while I dance amid the tedded hay
With merry maids, whose ringlets toss in light.

Or lies the purple evening on the bay
Of the calm glossy lake, O let me hide
   Unheard, unseen, behind the alder-trees,
For round their roots the fisher's boat is tied,
   On whose trim seat doth Edmund stretch at ease,
And while the lazy boat sways to and fro,
   Breathes in his flute sad airs, so wild and slow,
That his own cheek is wet with quiet tears.

But O, dear Anne! when midnight wind careers,
And the gust pelting on the out-house shed
  Makes the cock shrilly in the rainstorm crow,
  To hear thee sing some ballad full of woe,
Ballad of ship-wreck'd sailor floating dead,
  Whom his own true-love buried in the sands!
Thee, gentle woman, for thy voice remeasures
Whatever tones and melancholy pleasures
  The things of Nature utter; birds or trees,
Or moan of ocean-gale in weedy caves,
Or where the stiff grass mid the heath-plant waves,
  Murmur and music thin of sudden breeze.

# The Mad Monk

I heard a voice from Etna's side;
  Where o'er a cavern's mouth
  That fronted to the south
A chestnut spread its umbrage wide:
A hermit or a monk the man might be;
  But him I could not see:
And thus the music flow'd along,
In melody most like to old Sicilian song:

'There was a time when earth, and sea, and skies,
  The bright green vale, and forest's dark recess,
With all things, lay before mine eyes
  In steady loveliness:
But now I feel, on earth's uneasy scene,
  Such sorrows as will never cease; –
  I only ask for peace;
If I must live to know that such a time has been!'
A silence then ensued:
    Till from the cavern came
    A voice; – it was the same!
And thus, in mournful tone, its dreary plaint renew'd:

'Last night, as o'er the sloping turf I trod,
  The smooth green turf, to me a vision gave
Beneath mine eyes, the sod –
  The roof of Rosa's grave!

'My heart has need with dreams like these to strive,
    For, when I woke, beneath mine eyes I found
    The plot of mossy ground,
    On which we oft have sat when Rosa was alive. –
Why must the rock, and margin of the flood,
    Why must the hills so many flow'rets bear,
Whose colours to a *murder'd* maiden's blood,
    Such sad resemblance wear? –

'*I struck the wound*, – this hand of mine!
For Oh, thou maid divine,
    I lov'd to agony!
The youth whom thou call'd'st thine
    Did never love like me!

'Is it the stormy clouds above
    That flash'd so red a gleam?
    On yonder downward trickling stream? –
'Tis not the blood of her I love. –
The sun torments me from his western bed,
    Oh, let him cease for ever to diffuse
    Those crimson spectre hues!
Oh, let me lie in peace, and be for ever dead!'

Here ceas'd the voice. In deep dismay,
Down thro' the forest I pursu'd my way.

# The Picture
## Or the Lover's Resolution

Through weeds and thorns, and matted underwood
I force my way; now climb, and now descend
O'er rocks, or bare or mossy, with wild foot
Crushing the purple whorts; while oft unseen,
Hurrying along the drifted forest-leaves,
The scared snake rustles. Onward still I toil,
I know not, ask not whither! A new joy,
Lovely as light, sudden as summer gust,
And gladsome as the first-born of the spring,
Beckons me on, or follows from behind,
Playmate, or guide! The master-passion quelled,
I feel that I am free. With dun-red bark
The fir-trees, and the unfrequent slender oak,
Forth from this tangle wild of bush and brake
Soar up, and form a melancholy vault
High o'er me, murmuring like a distant sea.

Here Wisdom might resort, and here Remorse;
Here too the love-lorn man, who, sick in soul,
And of this busy human heart aweary,
Worships the spirit of unconscious life
In tree or wild-flower. – Gentle lunatic!
If so he might not wholly cease to be,
He would far rather not be that he is;
But would be something that he knows not of,
In winds or waters, or among the rocks!

But hence, fond wretch! breathe not contagion here!
No myrtle-walks are these: these are no groves
Where Love dare loiter! If in sullen mood
He should stray hither, the low stumps shall gore
His dainty feet, the briar and the thorn
Make his plumes haggard. Like a wounded bird

Easily caught, ensnare him, O ye Nymphs,
Ye Oreads chaste, ye dusky Dryades!
And you, ye Earth-winds! you that make at morn
The dew-drops quiver on the spiders' webs!
You, O ye wingless Airs! that creep between
The rigid stems of heath and bitten furze,
Within whose scanty shade, at summer-noon,
The mother-sheep hath worn a hollow bed –
Ye, that now cool her fleece with dropless damp,
Now pant and murmur with her feeding lamb.
Chase, chase him, all ye Fays, and elfin Gnomes!
With prickles sharper than his darts bemock
His little Godship, making him perforce
Creep through a thorn-bush on yon hedgehog's back.

   This is my hour of triumph! I can now
With my own fancies play the merry fool,
And laugh away worse folly, being free.
Here will I seat myself, beside this old,
Hollow, and weedy oak, which ivy-twine
Clothes as with net-work: here will I couch my limbs,
Close by this river, in this silent shade,
As safe and sacred from the step of man
As an invisible world – unheard, unseen,
And listening only to the pebbly brook
That murmurs with a dead, yet tinkling sound;
Or to the bees, that in the neighbouring trunk
Make honey-hoards. The breeze, that visits me,
Was never Love's accomplice, never raised
The tendril ringlets from the maiden's brow,
And the blue, delicate veins above her cheek;
Ne'er played the wanton – never half disclosed
The maiden's snowy bosom, scattering thence
Eye-poisons for some love-distempered youth,
Who ne'er henceforth may see an aspen-grove

Shiver in sunshine, but his feeble heart
Shall flow away like a dissolving thing.

Sweet breeze! thou only, if I guess aright,
Liftest the feathers of the robin's breast,
That swells its little breast, so full of song,
Singing above me, on the mountain-ash.
And thou too, desert stream! no pool of thine,
Though clear as lake in latest summer-eve,
Did e'er reflect the stately virgin's robe,
The face, the form divine, the downcast look
Contemplative! Behold! her open palm
Presses her cheek and brow! her elbow rests
On the bare branch of half-uprooted tree,
That leans towards its mirror! Who erewhile
Had from her countenance turned, or looked by stealth,
(For Fear is true-love's cruel nurse), he now
With steadfast gaze and unoffending eye,
Worships the watery idol, dreaming hopes
Delicious to the soul, but fleeting, vain,
E'en as that phantom-world on which he gazed,
But not unheeded gazed: for see, ah! see,
The sportive tyrant with her left hand plucks
The heads of tall flowers that behind her grow,
Lychnis, and willow-herb, and fox-glove bells:
And suddenly, as one that toys with time,
Scatters them on the pool! Then all the charm
Is broken – all that phantom world so fair
Vanishes, and a thousand circlets spread,
And each mis-shape the other. Stay awhile,
Poor youth, who scarcely dar'st lift up thine eyes!
The stream will soon renew its smoothness, soon
The visions will return! And lo! he stays:
And soon the fragments dim of lovely forms
Come trembling back, unite, and now once more
The pool becomes a mirror; and behold

Each wildflower on the marge inverted there,
And there the half-uprooted tree – but where,
O where the virgin's snowy arm, that leaned
On its bare branch? He turns, and she is gone!
Homeward she steals through many a woodland maze
Which he shall seek in vain. Ill-fated youth!
Go, day by day, and waste thy manly prime
In mad love-yearning by the vacant brook,
Till sickly thoughts bewitch thine eyes, and thou
Behold'st her shadow still abiding there,
The Naiad of the mirror!
                              Not to thee,
O wild and desert stream! belongs this tale:
Gloomy and dark art thou – the crowded firs
Spire from thy shores, and stretch across thy bed,
Making thee doleful as a cavern-well:
Save when the shy king-fishers build their nest
On thy steep banks, no loves hast thou, wild stream!

   This be my chosen haunt – emancipate
From Passion's dreams, a freeman, and alone,
I rise and trace its devious course. O lead,
Lead me to deeper shades and lonelier glooms.
Lo! stealing through the canopy of firs,
How fair the sunshine spots that mossy rock,
Isle of the river, whose disparted waves
Dart off asunder with an angry sound,
How soon to re-unite! And see! they meet,
Each in the other lost and found: and see
Placeless, as spirits, one soft water-sun
Throbbing within them, heart at once and eye!
With its soft neighbourhood of filmy clouds,
The stains and shadings of forgotten tears,
Dimness o'erswum with lustre! Such the hour
Of deep enjoyment, following love's brief feuds
And hark, the noise of a near waterfall!

I pass forth into light – I find myself
Beneath a weeping birch (most beautiful
Of forest trees, the Lady of the Woods),
Hard by the brink of a tall weedy rock
That overbrows the cataract. How bursts
The landscape on my sight! Two crescent hills
Fold in behind each other, and so make
A circular vale, and land-locked, as might seem,
With brook and bridge, and grey stone cottages,
Half hid by rocks and fruit-trees. At my feet,
The whortle-berries are bedewed with spray,
Dashed upwards by the furious waterfall.
How solemnly the pendent ivy-mass
Swings in its winnow: All the air is calm.
The smoke from cottage-chimneys, tinged with light,
Rises in columns; from this house alone,
Close by the water-fall, the column slants,
And feels its ceaseless breeze. But what is this?
That cottage, with its slanting chimney-smoke,
And close beside its porch a sleeping child,
His dear head pillowed on a sleeping dog –
One arm between its fore-legs, and the hand
Holds loosely its small handful of wild-flowers
Unfilletted, and of unequal lengths.
A curious picture, with a master's haste
Sketched on a strip of pinky-silver skin,
Peeled from the birchen bark! Divinest maid!
Yon bark her canvas, and those purple berries
Her pencil! See, the juice is scarcely dried
On the fine skin! She has been newly here;
And lo! yon patch of heath has been her couch –
The pressure still remains! O blessèd couch!
For this may'st thou flower early, and the sun,
Slanting at eve, rest bright, and linger long
Upon thy purple bells! O Isabel!
Daughter of genius! stateliest of our maids!

More beautiful than whom Alcaeus wooed,
The Lesbian woman of immortal song!
O child of genius! stately, beautiful,
And full of love to all, save only me,
And not ungentle e'en to me! My heart,
Why beats it thus? Through yonder coppice-wood
Needs must the pathway turn, that leads straightway
On to her father's house. She is alone!
The night draws on – such ways are hard to hit –
And fit it is I should restore this sketch,
Dropt unawares, no doubt. Why should I yearn
To keep the relique? 'twill but idly feed
The passion that consumes me. Let me haste!
The picture in my hand which she has left;
She cannot blame me that I followed her:
And I may be her guide the long wood through.

# The Pains of Sleep

Ere on my bed my limbs I lay,
It hath not been my use to pray
With moving lips or bended knees;
But silently, by slow degrees,
My spirit I to Love compose,
In humble trust mine eye-lids close,
With reverential resignation,
No wish conceived, no thought exprest,
Only a sense of supplication;
A sense o'er all my soul imprest
That I am weak, yet not unblest,
Since in me, round me, every where
Eternal Strength and Wisdom are.

But yester-night I prayed aloud
In anguish and in agony,
Up-starting from the fiendish crowd
Of shapes and thoughts that tortured me:
A lurid light, a trampling throng,
Sense of intolerable wrong,
And whom I scorned, those only strong!

Thirst of revenge, the powerless will
Still baffled, and yet burning still!
Desire with loathing strangely mixed
On wild or hateful objects fixed.
Fantastic passions! maddening brawl!
And shame and terror over all!
Deeds to be hid which were not hid,
Which all confused I could not know
Whether I suffered, or I did:
For all seemed guilt, remorse or woe,
My own or others still the same
Life-stifling fear, soul-stifling shame.

So two nights passed: the night's dismay
Saddened and stunned the coming day.
Sleep, the wide blessing, seemed to me
Distemper's worst calamity.
The third night, when my own loud scream
Had waked me from the fiendish dream,
O'ercome with sufferings strange and wild,
I wept as I had been a child;
And having thus by tears subdued
My anguish to a milder mood,
Such punishments, I said, were due
To natures deepliest stained with sin, –
For aye entempesting anew
The unfathomable hell within,
The horror of their deeds to view,
To know and loathe, yet wish and do!

# Recollections of Love

### I

How warm this woodland wild Recess!
  Love surely hath been breathing here;
  And this sweet bed of heath, my dear!
Swells up, then sinks with faint caress,
  As if to have you yet more near.

### II

Eight springs have flown, since last I lay
  On sea-ward Quantock's heathy hills,
  Where quiet sounds from hidden rills
Float here and there, like things astray,
  And high o'er head the sky-lark shrills.

### III

No voice as yet had made the air
  Be music with your name; yet why
  That asking look? that yearning sigh?
That sense of promise every where?
  Belovèd! flew your spirit by?

### IV

As when a mother doth explore
  The rose-mark on her long-lost child,
  I met, I loved you, maiden mild!
As whom I long had loved before –
  So deeply had I been beguiled.

### V

You stood before me like a thought,
  A dream remembered in a dream.
  But when those meek eyes first did seem
To tell me, Love within you wrought –
  O Greta, dear domestic stream!

## VI

Has not, since then, Love's prompture deep,
    Has not Love's whisper evermore
    Been ceaseless, as thy gentle roar?
Sole voice when other voices sleep,
    Dear under-song in clamor's hour.

# APPENDIX

# The Destiny of Nations
## A Vision

Auspicious Reverence! Hush all meaner song,
Ere we the deep preluding strain have poured
To the Great Father, only Rightful King.
Eternal Father! King Omnipotent!
To the Will Absolute, the One, the Good!
The I AM, the Word, the Life, the Living God!

   Such symphony requires best instrument.
Seize, then, my soul! from Freedom's trophied dome
The Harp which hangeth high between the Shields
Of Brutus and Leonidas! With that
Strong music, that soliciting spell, force back
Man's free and stirring spirit that lies entranced.
   For what is Freedom, but the unfettered use
Of all the powers which God for use had given?
But chiefly this, him First, him Last to view
Through meaner powers and secondary things
Effulgent, as through clouds that veil his blaze.
For all that meets the bodily sense I deem
Symbolical, one mighty alphabet
For infant minds; and we in this low world
Placed with our backs to bright Reality,
That we may learn with young unwounded ken
The substance from its shadow. Infinite Love,
Whose latence is the plenitude of All,
Thou with retracted beams, and self-eclipse
Veiling, revealest thine eternal Sun.

   But some there are who deem themselves most free
When they within this gross and visible sphere
Chain down the wingèd thought, scoffing ascent,
Proud in their meanness: and themselves they cheat
With noisy emptiness of learnèd phrase,

Their subtle fluids, impacts, essences,
Self-working tools, uncaused effects, and all
Those blind Omniscients, those Almighty Slaves,
Untenanting creation of its God.

   But Properties are God: the naked mass
(If mass there be, fantastic guess or ghost)
Acts only by its inactivity.
Here we pause humbly. Others boldlier think
That as one body seems the aggregate
Of atoms numberless, each organized;
So by a strange and dim similitude
Infinite myriads of self-conscious minds
Are one all-conscious Spirit, which informs
With absolute ubiquity of thought
(His one eternal self-affirming act!)
All his involvèd Monads, that yet seem
With various province and apt agency
Each to pursue its own self-centering end.
Some nurse the infant diamond in the mine;
Some roll the genial juices through the oak;
Some drive the mutinous clouds to clash in air,
And rushing on the storm with whirlwind speed,
Yoke the red lightnings to their volleying car.
Thus these pursue their never-varying course,
No eddy in their stream. Others, more wild,
With complex interests weaving human fates,
Duteous or proud, alike obedient all,
Evolve the process of eternal good.

   And what if some rebellious, o'er dark realms
Arrogate power? yet these train up to God,
And on the rude eye, unconfirmed for day,
Flash meteor-lights better than total gloom.
As ere from Lieule-Oaive's vapoury head
The Laplander beholds the far-off Sun
Dart his slant beam on unobeying snows,

While yet the stern and solitary Night
Brooks no alternate sway, the Boreal Morn
With mimic lustre substitutes its gleam,
Guiding his course or by Niemi lake
Or Balda Zhiok, or the mossy stone
Of Solfar-kapper, while the snowy blast
Drifts arrowy by, or eddies round his sledge,
Making the poor babe at its mother's back
Scream in its scanty cradle: he the while
Wins gentle solace as with upward eye
He marks the streamy banners of the North,
Thinking himself those happy spirits shall join
Who there in floating robes of rosy light
Dance sportively. For Fancy is the power
That first unsensualises the dark mind,
Giving it new delights; and bids it swell
With wild activity; and peopling air,
By obscure fears of Beings, invisible,
Emancipates it from the grosser thrall
Of the present impulse, teaching Self-control,
Till Superstition with unconscious hand
Seat Reason on her throne. Wherefore not vain,
Nor yet without permitted power impressed,
I deem those legends terrible, with which
The polar ancient thrills his uncouth throng:
Whether of pitying Spirits that make their moan
O'er slaughter'd infants, or that Giant Bird
Vuokho, of whose rushing wings the noise
Is Tempest, when the unutterable Shape
Speeds from the mother of Death and utters once
That shriek, which never murderer heard, and lived.

Or if the Greenland Wizard in strange trance
Pierces the untravelled realms of Ocean's bed
Over the abysm, even to that uttermost cave
By mis-shaped prodigies beleaguered, such

As Earth ne'er bred, nor Air, nor the upper Sea:
Where dwells the Fury Form, whose unheard name
With eager eye, pale cheek, suspended breath,
And lips half-opening with the dread of sound,
Unsleeping Silence guards, worn out with fear
Lest haply 'scaping on some treacherous blast
The fateful word let slip the Elements
And frenzy Nature. Yet the wizard her,
Arm'd with Torngarsuck's power, the Spirit of Good,
Forces to unchain the foodful progeny
Of the Ocean stream; – thence thro' the realm of Souls,
Where live the Innocent, as far from cares
As from the storms and overwhelming waves
That tumble on the surface of the Deep,
Returns with far-heard pant, hotly pursued
By the fierce Warders of the Sea, once more,
Ere by the frost foreclosed, to repossess
His fleshly mansion, that had staid the while
In the dark tent within a cow'ring group
Untenanted. – Wild phantasies! yet wise,
On the victorious goodness of high God
Teaching reliance, and medicinal hope,
Till from Bethabra northward, heavenly Truth
With gradual steps, winning her difficult way,
Transfer their rude Faith perfected and pure.

  If there be Beings of higher class than Man
I deem no nobler province they possess,
Than by disposal of apt circumstance
To rear up kingdoms: and the deeds they prompt,
Distinguishing from mortal agency,
They choose their human ministers from such states
As still the Epic song half fears to name,
Repelled from all the ministrelsies that strike
The palace-roof and soothe the monarch's pride.
And such, perhaps, the Spirit, who (if words

Witnessed by answering deeds may claim our faith)
Held commune with that warrior-maid of France
Who scourged the Invader. From her infant days,
With Wisdom, mother of retired thoughts,
Her soul had dwelt; and she was quick to mark
The good and evil thing, in human lore
Undisciplined. For lowly was her birth,
And Heaven had doomed her early years to toil
That pure from Tyranny's least deed, herself
Unfeared by Fellow-natures, she might wait
On the poor labouring man with kindly looks,
And minister refreshment to the tired
Way-wanderer, when along the rough-hewn bench
The sweltry man had stretched him, and aloft
Vacantly watched the rudely-pictured board
Which on the Mulberry-bough with welcome creak
Swung to the pleasant breeze. Here, too, the Maid
Learnt more than Schools could teach: Man's shifting mind,
His vices and his sorrows! And full oft
At tales of cruel wrong and strange distress
Had wept and shivered. To the tottering Eld
Still as a daughter would she run: she placed
His cold limbs at the sunny door, and loved
To hear him story, in his garrulous sort,
Of his eventful years, all come and gone.

So twenty seasons past. The Virgin's form,
Active and tall, nor Sloth nor Luxury
Had shrunk or paled. Her front sublime and broad,
Her flexile eye-brows wildly haired and low,
And her full eye, now bright, now unillumed,
Spake more than Woman's thought; and all her face
Was moulded to such features as declared
That Pity there had oft and strongly worked,
And sometimes Indignation. Bold her mien,
And like an haughty huntress of the woods

She moved: yet sure she was a gentle maid!
And in each motion her most innocent soul
Beamed forth so brightly, that who saw would say
Guilt was a thing impossible in her!
Nor idly would have said – for she had lived
In this bad World, as in a place of Tombs,
And touched not the pollutions of the Dead.

'Twas the cold season when the Rustic's eye
From the drear desolate whiteness of his fields
Rolls for relief to watch the skiey tints
And clouds slow-varying their huge imagery;
When now, as she was wont, the healthful Maid
Had left her pallet ere one beam of day
Slanted the fog-smoke. She went forth alone
Urged by the indwelling angel-guide, that oft,
With dim inexplicable sympathies
Disquieting the heart, shapes out Man's course
To the predoomed adventure. Now the ascent
She climbs of that steep upland, on whose top
The Pilgrim-man, who long since eve had watched
The alien shine of unconcerning stars,
Shouts to himself, there first the Abbey-lights
Seen in Neufchâtel's vale; now slopes adown
The winding sheep-track vale-ward: when, behold
In the first entrance of the level road
An unattended team! The foremost horse
Lay with stretched limbs; the others, yet alive
But stiff and cold, stood motionless, their manes
Hoar with the frozen night-dews. Dismally
The dark-red dawn now glimmered; but its gleams
Disclosed no face of man. The maiden paused,
Then hailed who might be near. No voice replied.
From the thwart wain at length there reached her ear
A sound so feeble that it almost seemed
Distant: and feebly, with slow effort pushed,

222

A miserable man crept forth: his limbs
The silent frost had eat, scathing like fire.
Faint on the shafts he rested. She, meantime,
Saw crowded close beneath the coverture
A mother and her children – lifeless all,
Yet lovely! not a lineament was marred –
Death had put on so slumber-like a form!
It was a piteous sight; and one, a babe,
The crisp milk frozen on its innocent lips,
Lay on the woman's arm, its little hand
Stretched on her bosom.

                              Mutely questioning,
The Maid gazed wildly at the living wretch.
He, his head feebly turning, on the group
Looked with a vacant stare, and his eye spoke
The drowsy calm that steals on worn-out anguish.
She shuddered; but, each vainer pang subdued,
Quick disentangling from the foremost horse
The rustic bands, with difficulty and toil
The stiff cramped team forced homeward. There arrived,
Anxiously tends him she with healing herbs,
And weeps and prays – but the numb power of Death
Spreads o'er his limbs; and ere the noon-tide hour,
The hovering spirits of his Wife and Babes
Hail him immortal! Yet amid his pangs,
With interruptions long from ghastly throes,
His voice had faltered out this simple tale.

   The Village, where he dwelt an husbandman,
By sudden inroad had been seized and fired
Late on the yester-evening. With his wife
And little ones he hurried his escape.
They saw the neighbouring hamlets flame, they heard
Uproar and shrieks! and terror-struck drove on
Through unfrequented roads, a weary way!
But saw nor house nor cottage. All had quenched

Their evening hearth-fire: for the alarm had spread.
The air clipt keen, the night was fanged with frost,
And they provisionless! The weeping wife
Ill hushed her children's moans; and still they moaned,
Till Fright and Cold and Hunger drank their life.
They closed their eyes in sleep, nor knew 'twas Death.
He only, lashing his o'er-wearied team,
Gained a sad respite, till beside the base
Of the hill his foremost horse dropped dead.
Then hopeless, strengthless, sick for lack of food,
He crept beneath the coverture, entranced,
Till wakened by the maiden. – Such his tale.

Ah! suffering to the height of what was suffered,
Stung with too keen a sympathy, the Maid
Brooded with moving lips, mute, startful, dark!
And now her flushed tumultuous features shot
Such strange vivacity, as fires the eye
Of Misery fancy-crazed! and now once more
Naked, and void, and fixed, and all within
The unquiet silence of confusèd thought
And shapeless feelings. For a mighty hand
Was strong upon her, till in the heat of soul
To the high hill-top tracing back her steps,
Aside the beacon, up whose smouldered stones
The tender ivy-trails crept thinly, there,
Unconscious of the driving element,
Yea, swallowed up in the ominous dream, she sate
Ghastly as broad-eyed Slumber! a dim anguish
Breathed from her look! and still with pant and sob,
Inly she toiled to flee, and still subdued,
Felt an inevitable Presence near.

Thus as she toiled in troublous ecstasy,
A horror of great darkness wrapt her round,
And a voice uttered forth unearthly tones,
Calming her soul, – 'O Thou of the Most High

Chosen, whom all the perfected in Heaven
Behold expectant –'

[The following fragments were intended to form part of the poem
when finished.]

'Maid beloved of Heaven!
(To her the tutelary Power exclaimed)
Of Chaos the adventurous progeny
Thou seest; foul missionaries of foul sire,
Fierce to regain the losses of that hour
When Love rose glittering, and his gorgeous wings
Over the abyss fluttered with such glad noise,
As what time after long and pestful calms,
With slimy shapes and miscreated life
Poisoning the vast Pacific, the fresh breeze
Wakens the merchant-sail uprising. Night
An heavy unimaginable moan
Sent forth, when she the Protoplast beheld
Stand beauteous on Confusion's charmèd wave.
Moaning she fled, and entered the Profound
That leads with downward windings to the Cave
Of Darkness palpable, Desert of Death
Sunk deep beneath Gehenna's massy roots.
There many a dateless age the Beldame lurked
And trembled; till engendered by fierce Hate,
Fierce Hate and gloomy Hope, a Dream arose,
Shaped like a black cloud marked with streaks of fire
It roused the Hell-Hag: she the dew-damp wiped
From off her brow, and through the uncouth maze
Retraced her steps; but ere she reached the mouth
Of that drear labyrinth, shuddering she paused,
Nor dared re-enter the diminished Gulph.
As through the dark vaults of some mouldered Tower
(Which, fearful to approach, the evening hind
Circles at distance in his homeward way)
The winds breathe hollow, deemed the plaining groan

225

Of prisoned spirits; with such fearful voice
Night murmured, and the sound through Chaos went.
Leaped at her call her hideous-fronted brood!
A dark behest they heard, and rushed on earth;
Since that sad hour, in Camps and Courts adored,
Rebels from God, and Tyrants o'er Mankind!'

\* \* \*

From his obscure haunt
Shrieked Fear, of Cruelty and ghastly Dam,
Feverous yet freezing, eager-paced yet slow,
As she that creeps from forth her swampy reeds,
Ague, the biform Hag! when early Spring
Beams on the marsh-bred vapours.
    'Even so (the exulting Maiden said)
The sainted Heralds of Good Tidings fell,
And thus they witnessed God! But now the clouds
Treading, and storms beneath their feet, they soar
Higher, and higher soar, and soaring sing
Loud songs of triumph! O ye Spirits of God,
Hover around my mortal agonies!'
She spake, and instantly faint melody
Melts on her ear, soothing and sad, and slow,
Such measures, as at calmest midnight heard
By agèd Hermit in his holy dream,
Foretell and solace death; and now they rise
Louder, as when with harp and mingled voice
The white-robed multitude of slaughtered saints
At Heaven's wide-open'd portals gratulant
Receive some martyred patriot. The harmony\*

---

\* Revelation 6: 9, 11: And when he had opened the fifth seal, I saw
under the altar the souls of them that were slain for the word of God
and for the Testimony which they held. And white robes were given
unto every one of them; and it was said unto them, that they should
rest yet for a little Season, until their fellow-servants also, and their
brethren that should be killed, as they were, should be fulfilled.

Entranced the Maid, till each suspendèd sense
Brief slumber seized, and confused ecstasy.

At length awakening slow, she gazed around:
And through a mist, the relict of that trance
Still thinning as she gazed, an Isle appeared,
Its high, o'er-hanging, white, broad-breasted cliffs,
Glassed on the subject ocean. A vast plain
Stretched opposite, where ever and anon
The plough-man following sad his meagre team
Turned up fresh sculls unstartled, and the bones
Of fierce hate-breathing combatants, who there
All mingled lay beneath the common earth,
Death's gloomy reconcilement! O'er the fields
Stept a fair Form, repairing all she might,
Her temples olive-wreathed; and where she trod,
Fresh flowerets rose, and many a foodful herb.
But wan her cheek, her footsteps insecure,
And anxious pleasure beamed in her faint eye,
As she had newly left a couch of pain,
Pale Convalescent! (Yet some time to rule
With power exclusive o'er the willing world,
That blessed prophetic mandate then fulfilled –
Peace be on Earth!) An happy while, but brief,
She seemed to wander with assiduous feet,
And healed the recent harm of chill and blight,
And nursed each plant that fair and virtuous grew.

But soon a deep precursive sound moaned hollow:
Black rose the clouds, and now (as in a dream),
Their reddening shapes, transformed to Warrior-hosts,
Coursed o'er the sky, and battled in mid-air.
Nor did not the large blood-drops fall from Heaven
Portentous! while aloft were seen to float,
Like hideous features looming on the mist,
Wan stains of ominous light! Resigned, yet sad,
The fair Form bowed her olive-crownèd brow,

Then o'er the plain with oft-reverted eye
Fled till a place of Tombs she reached, and there
Within a ruined Sepulchre obscure
Found hiding-place.
                    The delegated Maid
Gazed through her tears, then in sad tones exclaimed: –
'Thou mild-eyed Form! wherefore, ah! wherefore fled?
The Power of Justice like a name all light,
Shone from thy brow; but all they, who unblamed
Dwelt in thy dwellings, call thee Happiness.
Ah! why, uninjured and unprofited,
Should multitudes against their brethren rush?
Why sow they guilt, still reaping misery?
Lenient of care, thy songs, O Peace! are sweet,
As after showers the perfumed gale of eve,
That flings the cool drops on a feverous cheek;
And gay thy grassy altar piled with fruits.
But boasts the shrine of Dæmon War one charm,
Save that with many an orgie strange and foul,
Dancing around with interwoven arms,
The Maniac Suicide and Giant Murder
Exult in their fierce union! I am sad,
And know not why the simple peasants crowd
Beneath the Chieftains' standard!' Thus the Maid.

   To her the tutelary Spirit said:
'When Luxury and Lust's exhausted stores
No more can rouse the appetites of kings;
When the low flattery of their reptile lords
Falls flat and heavy on the accustomed ear;
When eunuchs sing, and fools buffoonery make,
And dancers writhe their harlot-limbs in vain;
Then War and all its dread vicissitudes
Pleasingly agitate their stagnant hearts;
Its hopes, its fears, its victories, its defeats,
Insipid Royalty's keen condiment!

*Therefore* uninjured and unprofited
(Victims at once and executioners),
The congregated Husbandmen lay waste
The vineyard and the harvest. As along
The Bothnic coast, or southward of the Line,
Though hushed the winds and cloudless the high noon,
Yet if Leviathan, weary of ease,
In sports unwieldy toss his island-bulk,
Ocean behind him billows, and before
A storm of waves breaks foamy on the strand.
And hence, for times and seasons bloody and dark,
Short Peace shall skin the wounds of causeless War,
And War, his strainèd sinews knit anew,
Still violate the unfinished works of Peace.
But yonder look! for more demands thy view!'
He said: and straightway from the opposite Isle
A vapour sailed, as when a cloud, exhaled
From Egypt's fields that steam hot pestilence,
Travels the sky for many a trackless league,
Till o'er some death-doomed land, distant in vain,
It broods incumbent. Forthwith from the plain,
Facing the Isle, a brighter cloud arose,
And steered its course which way the vapour went.

The Maiden paused, musing what this might mean.
But long time passed not, ere that brighter cloud
Returned more bright; along the plain it swept;
And soon from forth its bursting sides emerged
A dazzling form, broad-bosomed, bold of eye,
And wild her hair, save where with laurels bound.
Not more majestic stood the healing God,
When from his bow the arrow sped that slew
Huge Python. Shriek'd Ambition's giant throng,
And with them hissed the locust-fiends that crawled
And glittered in Corruption's slimy track.
Great was their wrath, for short they knew their reign;

And such commotion made they, and uproar,
As when the mad Tornado bellows through
The guilty islands of the western main,
What time departing from their native shores,
Eboe, or Koromantyn's plain of palms,
The infuriate spirits of the murdered make
Fierce merriment, and vengeance ask of Heaven.
Warmed with new influence, the unwholesome plain
Sent up its foulest fogs to meet the morn:
The Sun that rose on Freedom, rose in Blood!

  'Maiden beloved, and Delegate of Heaven!
(To her the tutelary Spirit said)
Soon shall the Morning struggle into Day,
The stormy Morning into cloudless Noon.
Much hast thou seen, nor all canst understand –
But this be thy best omen – save thy Country!'
Thus saying, from the answering Maid he passed,
And with him disappeared the heavenly Vision.

  'Glory to Thee, Father of Earth and Heaven!
All-conscious Presence of the Universe!
Nature's vast ever-acting Energy!
In will, in deed, Impulse of All to All!
Whether thy Love with unrefracted ray
Beam on the Prophet's purgèd eye, or if
Diseasing realms the Enthusiast, wild of thought,
Scatter new frenzies on the infected throng,
Thou both inspiring and predooming both,
Fit instruments and best, of perfect end:
Glory to Thee, Father of Earth and Heaven!'

\*   \*   \*

And first a landscape rose
More wild and waste and desolate than where
The white bear, drifting on a field of ice,
Howls to her sundered cubs with piteous rage
And savage agony.

# Index of First Lines